What Exactly is the Gospel?

A Guide for Born Again Christians to Share the
Good News of Jesus Christ

James Finke

JAMES FINKE READERS' CLUB

My free monthly email newsletter is packed with useful info to help you share the Good News of Jesus Christ with others. It contains deals and giveaways that aren't offered anywhere else, and you'll be the first to hear when new books in the series are released! Subscribers receive a welcome package that includes:

1. A free book of mine that is ONLY available to my readers' club.

2. A free audio download of the "You Don't Need a Ph.D. to Find G-O-D" message I delivered at my home church.

SUBSCRIBE

MORE BOOKS BY JAMES FINKE

Have you read the entire ***CHRISTIANITY UNCOM-PLICATED*** series?

This book distills and deciphers the evidence that the God of the Bible exists. Are you ready? Let's talk God.

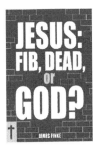

This book answers the most important question in history, asked by the most important person in history. Are you ready? Let's talk Jesus.

This book gives the business case for why we believe the Bible is the Word of God. Are you ready? Let's talk Bible.

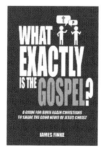

This book shares the most powerful message ever delivered on planet Earth. Let's talk Gospel.

Contents

INTRODUCTION

"I don't care what anyone says, but something isn't right about the world and how life is."

Yikes.

When I first came across this quote on a social media post, as expected, it was paired with cryptic music and a video of rain falling on a dark and dreary night in the background.

The post had gone viral. And while it wasn't something I'd normally be interested in; I was fascinated by how people reacted to the quote. Apparently, there are many out there who recognize that something indeed, "isn't right about the world and how life is."

As I write this book, the video has been viewed nearly 7 million times. Over 1.6 million people have "liked" it, and there have been over 42,000 comments left in the comment section. Out of the 42,000 responses, here are some of the most popular:

- *"Recently it feels like a fever dream. To be honest, one day I felt like it was a dream, and my original version is sick or something."* – "liked" by over 73,000 people.

- *"Everything just doesn't feel real anymore."* – "liked" by over 69,000 people.

- *"Anyone else's life going by so fast and you don't even remember the past few years?* – "liked" by over 62,000 people

- *"We are the only species that pays to live on this planet."* – "liked" by over 22,000 people.

- *"Has anyone else just been at their lowest all month?"* – "liked" by over 19,000 people.

- *"Been like it for a while, I'm so uncomfortable here."* – "liked" by over 15,000 people.

- *"The world feels dark, sad, depressing, gloomy and mysterious now. Wasn't what I remember before covid."* – "liked" by over 14,000 people.

- *"I've been feeling homesick like I'm not supposed to be here. Everywhere I go I don't feel welcome. Even my own home…"* – "liked" by over 5,000 people.

My dear Brothers and Sisters in Christ – doesn't this remind you of what we read in Matthew, Chapter 9?

> *"Then Jesus went about all the cities and villages, teaching in their synagogues, preaching the gospel of the kingdom, and healing every sickness and every disease among the people. But when He saw the multitudes, He was moved with compassion for them, because they were weary and scattered, like sheep*

having no shepherd. Then He said to His disciples, 'The harvest truly is plentiful, but the laborers are few. Therefore pray the Lord of the harvest to send out laborers into His harvest.'"[1]

We are surrounded today by people who are utterly lost. They are weary and scattered, like sheep having no shepherd. Jesus said it would be so. He said the harvest would be plentiful for laborers willing to go out into the world on His behalf. But for what?

To share the Gospel!

We know that absolutely nothing else will satisfy the longings of the human heart. If the pleasures of this world could satisfy it, then every rich, famous, and beautiful person in Hollywood would be living the perfect life. But God knows that's not true.

The importance of preaching the Gospel cannot be overstated because it is the hope for this world. This is a life and death issue – a heaven and hell issue. It's a direct command from Jesus, and it's literally why we are here on Earth.

To share the Gospel is both a privilege and an awesome responsibility. The Bible tells us to *"always be prepared to give an answer to everyone who asks you to give the reason for the hope that you have."*

Are you prepared?

The Gospel, translated as Good News, Good Announcement, or Good Message – is the good news about the person and work of Jesus Christ. I've found that many of us ostensibly understand the Gospel but may find it difficult to explain it to someone else. My prayer is that God would use this book to enhance your understanding, so that you are better prepared to share the good news with others.

Naturally, we're going to start "in the beginning..."

PART 1 - THIS IS THE GOSPEL

Chapter 1

IN THE BEGINNING...

What is the most serious problem in the world?

War? Disease? Poverty?

There is no shortage of choices. Here are today's headlines from one major news outlet:[2]

- Russia is 'torturing, kidnapping kids; Mariupol 'completely destroyed,' says Zelenskyy

- Experts warn Putin inching closer to North Korea with latest crackdown

- Monster tornado tears through Oklahoma, trapping residents in homes

- Kirby questioned on Russa war crimes and Iran nuclear deal revival

- Bad news for Americans hoping for lower gas prices

- Feminist organizations stay mum after transgender swimmer dominates women's championship

- As her relatives fight for freedom, Ukrainian owner of Russian restaurant inundated with hate

- Think your grocery bill is high now? Experts warn just wait.

- St. Louis prosecutors will not charge man arrested for trying to carjack police officers

- Wallets, IDs but no survivors found after China Eastern plane crash

- Economists sound the alarm on 1970's-style catastrophe

- We have a right to know what's going on in Ukraine, but our leaders are lying

- Miami Beach imposes curfew to deal with spring breakers after shootings

- Health officials sound the alarm over new Omnicron subvariant

It's almost unbelievable, but this is a single day's headlines from a single news outlet. As grave as this list is, it's far from comprehensive. There are countless other causes of human suffering that are occurring right now as we speak. So, what do people actually believe is the single most serious problem on Earth? To attempt to answer this question, the World Economic Forum conducted a survey, and according to millennials, the ten most concerning issues in the world are as follows: [3]

10. Unemployment

9. Safety

8. Lack of education

7. Food and water security

6. Government corruption

5. Religious conflicts

4. Poverty

3. Inequality

2. War

1. Climate change

Indeed, these are enormous problems. This "Top 10" list seems mostly reasonable.

It's also unequivocally and completely wrong.

These issues are *temporary* worldly symptoms of an infinitely greater *eternal* spiritual problem. Actually, there's nothing wrong with treating the symptoms. We're right do it. But if we never address the true problem, all we've done is make our brief time on Earth a little more pleasant.

My Pastor describes this as a "fruit versus root" problem. If you knock the apples off an apple tree, it will look different for a little while. But nothing has really changed because you only addressed the fruit. There will be new apples on that tree in the next season. So to actually change the tree, we need to address the root.

If you really think about it, you will notice that the problems on that list are fruit. For example, if we completely eliminated global warming, the world's most concerning problem, would your life be perfect? Of course not. And that goes for every item on the list. Would life be perfect if there were no unemployment, war, or poverty? Still no. You and I both know that even if we somehow did the impossible and eliminated all of these problems, humans would still find ways to disagree and inflict harm on each other. Finally, how could we enjoy life on Earth knowing that all is lost after we die?

We can't.

And that is why when we only address the problems of the world, it's like taking Tylenol when you need a heart transplant. It may help us feel a little better for a while, but we're missing the exact solution.

We need to quite literally go to the root. Let's read:

In the beginning, God created the heavens and earth. He said 'let there be light' and there was light. And God saw the light, that it was good.

Then God said, "Let the waters under the heavens be gathered together into one place, and let the dry land appear"... and it was good.

Then God said, "Let the earth bring forth grass, the herb that yields seed, and the fruit tree that yields fruit according to its kind... and it was good.

Then God said, "Let there be lights in the firmament of the heavens to divide the day from the night; and let them be for signs and seasons, and for days and years; and let them be for lights in the firmament of the heavens to give light on the earth"... and it was good.

Then God said, "Let the waters abound with an abundance of living creatures, and let birds fly above the earth across the face of the firmament of the heavens."... and it was good.

Then God said, "Let the earth bring forth the living creature according to its kind: cattle and creeping thing and beast of the earth, each according to its kind"... and it was good.

Then God said, "Let Us make man in Our image, according to Our likeness; let them have dominion over the fish of the sea, over the birds of the air, and over the cattle, over all the earth and over every creeping thing that creeps on the earth." So God created man in His own image; in the image of God He created him; male and female He created them. Then God blessed them, and God said to them, "Be fruitful and multiply; fill the earth and subdue it; have dominion over the fish of the sea, over the birds of the air, and over every living thing that moves on the earth." Then God saw everything that He had made, and indeed it was very good

In summary: when God created our world, it was good at all levels. It's this truth that guides us to the very root of our problem:

How did we go from "it was very good" to... this?

Well, we know exactly what happened. So, let's keep going...

Chapter 2

THE FIRST SIN

How did our world go from "it was very good" to... this? Thankfully, the Bible records "The Fall" of humanity, and this passage recounts the first sin – the *Original Sin.*

"Now the serpent was more cunning than any beast of the field which the Lord God had made. And he said to the woman, 'Has God indeed said, 'You shall not eat of every tree of the garden'?' And the woman said to the serpent, 'We may eat from the fruit of the trees of the garden; but of the fruit of the tree which is in the midst of the garden, God has said, 'You shall not eat it, nor shall you touch it, lest you die.' Then the serpent said to the woman, 'You will not surely die. For God knows that in the day you eat of it your eyes will be opened, and you will be like God, knowing good and evil. So when the woman saw that the tree was good for food, that it was pleasant to the eyes, and a tree desirable to make one wise, she took of its fruit and ate. She also gave it to her husband with her, and he ate... therefore the Lord God sent him out of the garden of Eden to till the ground from which he was taken. So He drove out the man; and He placed

cherubim at the east of the garden of Eden, and a flaming sword which turned every way, to guard the way to the tree of life." [4]

Now – there's a fair chance you've heard something like this before from skeptics, "Whoa, whoa. You don't actually believe that there was a talking snake in an actual garden of Eden, do you?" Perhaps you've even questioned whether this was an actual historical event, just symbolic, or some combination of the two. It's an understandable question for an account that includes elements like the serpent (Satan), the tree of life, the tree of knowledge of good and evil, etc.

There is no question that there is symbolism in the narrative. For instance, Adam literally means "man" in Hebrew. God created Adam (God created man). That said, according to world-class Bible scholar William Lane Craig, there are solid Biblical grounds to believe that Adam and Eve were actual historical people. Craig describes "The Fall" as "a historical event that actually happened, though it is told in a dramatic literary form involving figurative speech."

There is no reason to deny the reality of the first sin committed by Adam and Eve. Therefore, when we share the Gospel, it's imperative that we get to what the doctrine of this Original Sin actually entails. We risk missing this critical point if we get hung up on what's literal vs. what's symbolic in the text. Let's read:

"Therefore, just as through one man sin entered the world, and death through sin, and thus death spread to all men, because all sinned... Therefore, as through one man's offense judgment came to all men, resulting in condemnation... For as one man's disobedience many were made sinners." [5]

Original Sin says that (through Adam and Eve) sin entered the world and is now *inevitable* for all humans. It refers to consequences for the entire human race. Human nature is now corrupt, with every one of us having evil impulses and desires.

And if they're still not sure about the doctrine of Original Sin, I recommend using a simple 2-part test:

Part 1. External- Original Sin says that sin is inevitable for all humans. Therefore, the obvious question is, do you know of anyone whose every thought, intent, and action has been perfect since birth? Of course not. Pastor Voddie Baucham quips that you must not have children if you don't believe in the Original Sin. Every parent knows that their children don't need to be taught to sin, but they live in sin. There is humor in the statement, but the reality is that everyone we've ever known on this planet is an imperfect sinner. That is directly consistent with the doctrine of Original Sin.

Part 2. Internal- let's now turn our attention to you. After "The Fall," the Bible records, *"Then the Lord saw the wickedness of man was great in the earth and that every intent of the thoughts of his heart was evil contin ually."*[6] That sounds absurd, right? Imagine there was a video compiled of every passing thought you've ever had on Earth. Now, how would you feel about playing that same video in a theater packed with your family, relatives, friends, co-workers, etc., watching closely? Something tells me you'd do whatever you could to prevent that movie from airing. What if we restricted it to every thought you've had in the past year? Or the past week? Or even the past 24 hours? You'd still be desperate to stop it from airing because human nature has been corrupt and bent toward evil since "The Fall." Again, this is directly consistent with the doctrine of Original Sin.[7]

My dear brothers and sisters in Christ, the effects of the Original Sin are *obvious* in our lives and the lives of everyone we've ever known. Sin is inevitable for all humans due to our fallen nature. The scripture is clear:

As it is written: There is no one righteous, not even one.[8]

It should also be noted that this isn't something new. You and I can relate to this passage, written nearly 2,000 years ago.

"I do not understand what I do. For what I want to do I do not do, but what I hate I do... For I have the desire to do what is good, but I cannot carry it out. For I do not do the good I want to do, but he evil I do not want to do- this I keep on doing. Now if I do what I do not want to do, it is no longer I who do it, but it is sin living in me that does it."[9]

Ok – so every one of us is a sinner. We're all in the same boat, just trying to do the best we can. So, what's the problem with that?

Well... to answer that question, we're going to look at what's been referred to as "the most terrifying truth in scripture." Let's go.

Chapter 3

THE MOST TERRIFYING TRUTH IN SCRIPTURE

The doctrine of Original Sin explains the reality that sin is inevitable for everyone. The entire human race has inherited a sinful and evil nature from Adam and Eve.

But at least we're all in the same boat, right? Sin is in our nature, and we're just doing the best we can under the circumstances. What's so bad about that?

The truth is that sin really isn't a very big deal. That is... unless you believe what the Bible says about God. If you believe what the Bible says about God, then you know that being a sinner is catastrophic. It is, by far, the worst problem in your life and mine.

That's why what I'm about to share has been referred to as the most terrifying truth in scripture.[10] Are you ready? Here it goes...

God is holy.

Now, it may not immediately be apparent to unbelievers (and perhaps even many believers) why it is so terrifying that God is Holy. If that's the case, it is most likely because they are unfamiliar with what it means to be Holy. **First, we must recognize that the Bible emphasizes God's holiness differently than any of His other attributes.** Let's read from one of the best-known passages in all of scripture:

Isaiah's Commission

"In the year that King Uzziah died, I saw the Lord, high and exalted, seated on a throne; and the train of his robe filled the temple. Above him were seraphim, each with six wings: With two wings they covered their faces, with two they covered their feet, and with two they were flying. And they were calling to one another: 'Holy, holy, holy is the Lord Almighty; the whole earth is full of his glory!'" -Isaiah 6: 1-3 NIV

Reading this scripture, you feel the magnificence in the passage. The Prophet Isaiah's vision brings him into the throne room and presence of the Lord. There, he sees the seraphim (angels), who God has created with the exact features they need to exist in His presence. They have two wings covering their faces because He is too pure and too glorious to be looked upon directly. They have two extra wings covering their feet because they stand on Holy ground. The remaining two wings are used to fly.

As they hover in the throne room, they're calling to each other, "Holy, holy, holy is the Lord Almighty; the whole Earth is full of His glory." This

"Holy, holy, holy" proclamation is absolutely remarkable. In English, we might use **bold**, *italics*, or ALL CAPS to emphasize a point. But in the Hebrew language, one of the ways they would draw particular emphasis on a word would be to say something twice in a row. For example, *"But even if we or an angel from heaven should preach a gospel other than the one we have preached you, let them be under God's curse. As we have already said, so now I say again: If anybody is preaching to you a gospel other than what you accepted, let them be under God's curse!"*[11]

We find this repetition used sparingly in scripture and reserved for instances where the author is hammering home a critical point. Now, keep in mind that's when something is repeated twice. In this case, the seraphim's cry is repeated three times! "Holy, Holy, Holy is the Lord Almighty." It's only in the most exceptional and rare circumstances that this 3x repetition would be used. In today's parlance, that would be like writing, "God is Holy!!!!!!" And this proclamation is being called out in the presence of the Lord in His throne room for eternity.

He is Holy.

No other attribute of God is emphasized in this way in the Bible. And just look how Jesus reinforces the point:

Now Jesus was praying in a certain place, and when He finished, one of His disciples said to Him, "Lord, teach us to pray, as John taught his disciples." And He said to them, "When you pray, say:

'Father, hallowed be your name. *Your kingdom come. Give us each our daily bread, and forgive us our sins, for we ourselves* *forgive everyone who is indebted to us. And lead us not into temptation. "*[12]

This passage, "The Lord's Prayer," is certainly familiar to you. Growing up, I recited this prayer thousands of times, yet I never really understood it. To explain, **to hallow means "to honor as holy."** In other words, the very first thing Jesus teaches us to pray is that God's name be honored as holy!

He is holy.

So, what's the problem? If God is referred to as Holy in scripture, then why is that "the most terrifying truth in scripture?"

Well, many believe that calling God holy is interchangeable with calling Him righteous, just, or pure. And He indeed is all of those things.

- He is pure- *Your eyes are too pure to approve evil, and you cannot look on wickedness with favor.*[4]

- He is just- *He is the Rock, His work is perfect, For all His ways are justice; a God of truth and without injustice, Righteous and upright is He.*[5]

- He is righteous- *Clouds and thick darkness surround Him [as at Sinai], Righteousness and justice are the foundation of His throne.*[6]

Scripture is clear that we serve a pure, righteous, and just God, but that is *not* what it means when the Bible says that He is holy.

It means that he is separate.

Holy is defined as "separate, unique, other." What the Bible is saying is that God is separate from everything that is sinful and evil.

This is the message we have heard from him and declare to you: God is light, in Him there is no darkness at all.[16]

Do you understand our problem now?

It's terrifying that God is holy because we are not. Just look at Isaiah's reaction to this revelation:

> *"In the year that King Uzziah died, I saw the Lord, high and exalted, seated on a throne; and the train of his robe filled the temple. Above him were seraphim, each with six wings: With two wings they covered their faces, with two they covered their feet, and with two they were flying. And they were calling to one another: 'Holy, holy, holy is the Lord Almighty; the whole earth is full of his glory! And the foundations of the thresholds shook at the voice of him who called, and the house was filled with smoke. **And I said: 'Woe is me! For I am lost; for I am a man of unclean lips; for my eyes have seen the King, the Lord of Hosts!'"***

The same thing happens when it's revealed to the Apostle Peter that Jesus, God the Son, is holy:

> *On one occasion, while the crowd was pressing in on him to hear the word of God, he was standing by the lake of Genneraset, and he saw two boats by the lake, but the fishermen had gone out of them and were washing their nets. Getting into one of the boats, which was Simon's, he asked him to put out a little from*

the land. And he sat down and taught the people from the boat. And when he had finished speaking, he said to Simon, 'Put out into the deep and let down your nets for a catch.' And Simon answered, 'Master, we toiled all night and took nothing! But at your word I will let down the nets.' And when they had done this, they enclosed a large number of fish, and their nets were breaking. They signaled to their partners in the other boat to come and help them. And they came and filled both the boats, so that they began to sink. ***But when Simon Peter saw it, he fell down at Jesus' knees saying, 'Depart from me, for I am a sinful man, O Lord.'***

These reactions illustrate the problem:

- You and I are sinful and evil (Original Sin)

- God is separate from everything that is sinful and evil (He is Holy)

Let's look at where that leaves us...

Chapter 4

GOD-SHAPED HOLE

S in led to a separation between a Holy God and sinful humanity.

Surely the arm of the Lord is not too short to save, nor his ear too dull to hear. But your iniquities have separated you from your God. Your sins have hidden His face from you, so that He will not hear.[17]

This separation is exactly why so many believe that "something isn't right about the world and how life is." The separation from our Creator has created a "God-shaped hole" in our hearts. Whether someone recognizes or overlooks the problem, we are all affected because every one of us is a sinner.

That is why our natural reaction is to try and fix it with the pleasures of the world. We seek fulfillment from something other than God. It may be something seemingly positive like making memories with our family, achieving goals, accumulating knowledge, earning money, doing good deeds, excelling in sports, etc., or it could be destructive habits like casual sex, drug abuse, alcohol abuse, etc.

Here's the reality: nothing in this world can satisfy our longing to be reconciled with the God who created us. Whether it's money, sex, destructive habits, relationships, or even good deeds, none would satisfy.

Even the healthiest, most enjoyable, most wonderful things this life has to offer will leave us dissatisfied if we put them in "first place" in our lives. Those things cannot fill the "God-shaped hole" in our hearts. We cannot escape the reality that we are sinners who are separated from our God.

And this problem during our brief time on Earth is only the tip of the iceberg, because we were made for so much more. The Bible tells us that God made us for eternity.

> *He has made everything beautiful in its time. He has also set eternity in the human heart; yet no one can fathom what God has done from beginning to end.*[18]

Now the question is, what happens if we remain separate from our God for eternity? In short, an eternity spent with God is in heaven, and an eternity spent apart from God is in hell.

> *For you are not a God who takes pleasure in wickedness. No evil can dwell with You.*[19]

Now, some people believe that God is too "nice" to create a place called hell. Only about 60% of US adults believe that hell exists (about 70% believe heaven exists).[20] Their reasoning for disputing the existence of hell is to point out Jesus' wise moral teachings on love and forgiveness. Therefore, it may surprise them to know that Jesus Christ, the Prince of Peace, preached about hell even more than He preached about heaven in the Bible.[21] He preached about His 2nd coming to judge the nations and warned us to escape the everlasting punishment, darkness, pain, and fire of hell.

Then He will also say to those on the left hand, 'Depart from Me, you cursed, into the everlasting fire prepared for the devil and his angels: for I was hungry and you gave Me no food; I was thirsty and you gave Me no drink; I was a stranger and you did not take Me in, naked and you did not clothe Me, sick and in prison and you did not visit Me.' "Then they also will answer Him, saying, 'Lord, when did we see You hungry or thirsty or a stranger or naked or sick or in prison, and did not minister to You?' Then He will answer them, saying, 'Assuredly, I say to you, inasmuch as you did not do it to one of the least of these, you did not do it to Me.' And these will go away into everlasting punishment, but the righteous into eternal life.[22]

But I say to you that everyone who [so much as] looks at a woman with lust for her has already committed adultery with her in his heart. If your right eye makes you stumble and leads you to sin, tear it out and throw it away [that is, remove yourself from the source of temptation]; for it is better for you to lose one of the parts of your body, than for your whole body to be thrown into hell.[23]

But the sons of the kingdom will be cast out into outer darkness. There will be weeping and gnashing of teeth.[24]

And do not fear those who kill the body but cannot kill the soul. But rather fear Him who is able to destroy both soul and body in hell.[25]

But I say to you that whoever is angry with his brother without a cause shall be in danger of the judgment. And whoever says to his brother, 'Raca!' shall be in danger of the council. But whoever says, 'You fool!' shall be in danger of hell fire.[26]

My brothers and sisters in Christ: I realize the topic of hell may make some people uncomfortable, particularly unbelievers. But we must deliver the truth of the good news of Jesus Christ (The Gospel) and the repercussions of sin with love and compassion to everyone.

Now, the unbelievers that you witness to may be thinking, "How can this be? I'm not so bad; I don't deserve to go to hell." But that begs the question: if you're confident that you don't "deserve" to go to hell, what specifically are the requirements to go to heaven instead? Let's look at God's standard and see how we measure up…

Chapter 5

BE YE PERFECT

Aside from the atheists, the vast majority of people you witness to will say that they believe they are going to heaven and not hell. They may spend their entire life here on earth ignoring, rejecting, or remaining undecided about God, yet at the same time, they expect to spend eternity with Him.

Why?

Most of them will say they believe they're going to heaven because of something like this: "I'm a pretty good guy. I do my best to be a good person."

In other words, most have no idea about the standards for acceptance into heaven. They believe they are going to heaven based on how they compare to *other people*. Other *"worse"* people. When we compare ourselves to other people, we can just about always come out looking pretty good. As an extreme example, even a onetime murderer could look relatively decent if compared to a mass murderer like Hitler. So, we tell ourselves that hell is reserved only for the other "worse" people. But the Bible says otherwise:

> *For we dare not class ourselves or compare ourselves with those*
> *who commend themselves. But they, measuring themselves by*

*themselves, and comparing themselves among themselves, are
not wise.*[27]

Unbelievers assume they are going to heaven because they have no con-
stant and real standard to measure themselves with. As Ray Comfort put it,
"What he tolerates today, he accepts tomorrow." People assume that God's
standards are the same as theirs. But again, scripture says otherwise:

> *These things you have done, and I kept silent; You thought that
> I was altogether like you, But I will rebuke you, And set them
> in order before your eyes.*[28]

> *And He (Jesus) said to them, "You are those who justify your-
> selves before men, but God knows your hearts. For what is highly
> esteemed among men is an abomination in the sight of God.*[29]

Would you expect a 100% acceptance rate if you undertook the following
endeavors?

- Applied to the most prestigious medical school in the world.

- Applied to the most prestigious engineering school in the world.

- Applied to the most prestigious law school in the world.

- Auditioned for a Broadway musical.

- Auditioned for Cirque de Soleil.

- Tried out for the New York Yankees.

- Tried out for the New England Patriots.

Of course not. You wouldn't qualify for all (or, more likely, any) of these institutions. It's not because they're mean, but you simply don't meet their rightfully and extremely high standards for acceptance.

Now, keep in mind that these are human institutions. They are literally *nothing* compared to the Kingdom of God. Therefore, it makes no sense to assume that the standard to spend eternity in the presence of a Holy and righteous God is lower than those of the world.

Thankfully, we don't have to guess what God's standard is. We know that He has revealed it to us in the Bible.

God's standard is "the law."

The Bible describes the law as holy, just, good, and perfect (Psalm 19:7, Romans 7:12). The law is "condensed into the Ten Commandments and is the summation of all moral and ethical laws."[30] Let's recap:[31]

1. *You shall have no other gods before Me* (to put anyone or anything in "first place" in your life before God)

2. *You shall not make for yourself any carved image* (to idolize someone other than God)

3. *You shall not take the name of the Lord your God in vain*

4. *Remember the Sabbath day* (to ignore Sunday as a holy day)

5. *Honor your father and your mother*

6. *You shall not murder*

7. You shall not commit adultery

8. You shall not steal

9. You shall not bear false witness against your neighbor (to lie)

10. You shall not covet. (to be envious of others' possessions)

Most unbelievers are familiar with the Ten Commandments, but a smaller percentage of them are aware of what the Bible actually says about them. Specifically, about how they are binding for every one of us. About how we'll be judged by them as God's standard to go to heaven. It's therefore very critical that we convey these truths regarding the commandments:

- **All of humanity is under the law**- *Now all has been heard; here is the conclusion of the matter: Fear God and keep his commandments, for this is the duty of all mankind.* [6]

- **If you break even one commandment one time, you are guilty of all**- *For whoever keeps the whole law and yet stumbles at just one point is guilty of breaking all of it.*[7]

- **Breaking the commandments brings about God's righteous anger**- *The law brings wrath.*[8]

- **Those guilty of breaking the law are under a curse**- *For all who rely on the works of the law are under a curse, as it is written: "Cursed is everyone who does not continue to do everything written in the Book of the Law.* [9]

Everyone is under the law and is obligated to obey the law. Have you ever broken a single one of the above commandments? That is, have you ever lied, stolen something, used the Lord's name in a derogatory way, spent your Sundays on personal projects, or even disrespected your parents?

The Bible says that if you've ever committed one of these sins once, you're guilty of breaking the entire law and are under a curse. In other words, you're not eligible for heaven.

Adam and Eve perpetrated "the ultimate act of adultery" and severed their relationship with the living God when they committed the first sin.[36] They were cast out of the presence of God, and a curse was said over all humanity because of their *one sin*.

That's one sin. How many times have you broken a commandment in your lifetime? Thousands? More?

But it gets better (or worse, depending on your perspective!) Jesus Christ explicitly said that it's not enough to abstain from committing these sins. We are guilty if we've even ever thought about doing these things on the inside. Listen to this:

> *You have heard it said that "You shall not commit adultery."*
> *But I tell you that anyone who even looks upon a woman lust-*
> *fully has already committed adultery with her in his heart.* [37]

Gulp.

And here comes the cherry on top. The Bible tells us that the law is our "tutor" that was added until the seed (Jesus) came to fulfill and personify the law.[38]

Jesus Christ came not to abolish the law but to fulfill it.[39] He lived a perfect life in accordance with the law. **It means for you to follow the law completely and qualify for heaven, you must be as perfect as Jesus Christ.** Jesus Himself said, "Be perfect, therefore, as your heavenly Father is perfect."[40]

In summary:

1. If you've ever broken a single commandment once in your life, you're guilty of all and under a curse.

2. If you've ever thought about breaking a single commandment once in your life, you're guilty of all and under a curse.

3. Unless you are as perfect as Jesus Christ, you are guilty and under a curse.

At this point, I would expect most (or all) unbelievers to exclaim that this is impossible and that no one could ever live up to that standard.

And that is precisely the point! The purpose of the law is to show us what God's holy standard is and that we cannot get there in our fallen state.

> *Therefore, no one will be declared righteous in God's sight by the works of the law; rather, through the law we become conscious of our sin.*[41]

We are all born with the moral law of God written on our hearts.[42] God gave the law so that our understanding of sin would increase.[43] **It shows us that we have absolutely no chance of earning our way into heaven by "doing our best to be a good person."**[44] We would have to live perfectly as Jesus Christ.

God provides this as the ultimate wake-up call for sinners (all of us). Sinners need to understand the inescapable result of breaking God's law. As soon as we realize we are utterly incapable of upholding God's holy law, we recognize that judgment, guilt, and condemnation await us. This realization motivates us to find an escape before it is too late. As John

MacArthur explains, "The fear of God is a necessary truth to drive sinners to seek reconciliation. With no fear of God, sinners go blindly to hell." Likewise, Charles Spurgeon explained, "they will never accept grace until they tremble before a just and holy law."

This motivation to be reconciled with God leads us to the greatest problem in the Bible.[45] Let's go...

Chapter 6

THE GREATEST PROBLEM IN THE BIBLE

T he Bible teaches that there is just one response to sin encountered by a Holy God: wrath (righteous anger).

Your eyes are too pure to look upon evil, and you cannot tolerate wrongdoing.[46]

You hate all who do iniquity.[47]

"Whoa, whoa, whoa," the skeptic may say. "I thought God was love? If God is love, He cannot hate." Well, they're mistaken. The truth is that God is love, and therefore, He must hate evil.

If you love what is right, true, and good, there is hostility against all that violates it.

"For I, the Lord, love justice; I hate robbery and wrongdoing."[48]

Pastor Paul Washer elaborates on this principle with these examples:

- I love babies, and therefore I must hate abortion.

- I love Jews, and therefore I must hate the holocaust.

- I love African Americans, and therefore I must hate slavery.

Every time we break the commandments, we rekindle the righteous anger of God that leads to judgment. He, therefore, condemns our evil doings because He is Holy.

"People are destined to die once, and after that to face judgment."[49]

"But because of your stubbornness and your unrepentant heart, you are storing up wrath against yourself for the day of God's wrath, when His righteous judgment will be revealed."[50]

Yikes.

When unbelievers are faced with this reality, they question the goodness of God. "Isn't your God supposed to be good and forgiving? How could He be a loving God but send everyone who sins to hell?"

To address this issue, we're going to take a quick trip back to 1980s Chicago. There was a curious situation that occurred within the court system. Consider this:[51]

- In 1980, Wilfredo Rosario confessed to a double murder. However, his honest confession was set aside, and he was found not guilty.

- That same year, William Chin was shot and killed in Chicago's Chinatown. Lenny Chow, a New York hit man for the On Leong mafia, was arrested and tried for murder. Surprisingly, He was also found not guilty.

- Owen Jones was accused of beating a man to death with a pipe during a burglary. He went to trial in 1982, where his charges were reduced from felony murder to voluntary manslaughter. As a result, he received a nine-year sentence in prison instead of the twenty-year sentence that the former would have produced.

What's the common thread among these three cases?

Judge Thomas J. Maloney.

In short, guilty mobsters knew they could secure a "not guilty" verdict if they were willing to pay Judge Maloney's "fee."

Evidently, this particular brand of "justice" is frowned upon by the FBI. Hence, Judge Maloney was indicted in 1991 following a 3 ½ year investigation. He was then convicted in April 1993 of accepting over $100,000 in bribes in exchange for acquittals and reduced sentences. Jurors said his habit of buying hundreds of money orders with cash convinced them of his guilt.[52] Today, the Judiciary Report lists Judge Maloney as one of the "Worst Judges in History."[53]

Strangely, there is a life-changing principle that we can learn from Judge Maloney:

Pardoning guilty sinners doesn't make a judge "good, loving, or nice" – it makes him corrupt.

Imagine it was one of your family members that was brutally murdered. The killer is rightly convicted, but at the sentencing, the judge says, "I am good, loving, and nice, so I am going to pardon you, sir. You're free to go." Obviously, anyone would be outraged. Humans are obsessed with rights and justice because we are created in the image of a righteous and just God.

Brothers and Sisters in Christ, the unbelievers we witness to need to know that this is basically what the entire Bible is about. It's called the greatest problem in the Bible:[54]

It is this:

If God is good, He cannot forgive you.

Do you see the rub? Everyone is guilty of breaking God's holy law, and the sentence is condemnation to hell. That's why the Bible says that the wages of sin is death.[55] Countless sinners misassume God will pardon them because He is "nice." But nice judges don't just pardon guilty sinners; corrupt ones also do. God isn't corrupt because He is Holy and righteous.

So, how can the Bible declare that God is both "just and the justifier of wicked men"?[56] How do we reconcile these two passages?

> *He is just - Acquitting the guilty and condemning the innocent – the Lord detests them both.*[57]

> *He forgives sinners (us!) - "As far as the east is from the west, so far has He removed our transgressions from us."*[58]

This is what it's all about. If God is a good judge, how can we possibly be forgiven? His righteousness demands punishment for all sin.

There is only one answer to that question, and it is found in the cross of Jesus Christ. Let's go.

Chapter 7

THE MESSIAH

How can God forgive sinners but still be a good judge? In a word, the answer is *Christ*. Sadly, just mentioning the word "Christ" will cause some unbelievers to recoil. Many have hardened their hearts against Christ (and, by extension, Christianity) because they personally know nothing about Him. They've been exposed to some distorted version of Christianity through many avenues like false prophets, churches, TV, the internet, or otherwise. They may instantly show disinterest and put up their defenses, telling you that they already know about Jesus and the church.

Most people who say these things have never heard the true Gospel! They know very little about Christ – who He is and what He's accomplished. So let's break it down.

God promised the nation of Israel that He would deliver a Savior - a righteous High Priest and King of kings who would sit on the throne forever.[59] This Savior is referred to as the "Messiah."

Jesus is this Messiah – hence the title Jesus Christ. Christ is simply the English version of the Greek term "Messiah."

Now, why would someone need a Savior in the first place? Simply put – it is those who cannot save themselves who need a Savior, and this is the entire purpose of this book. Brothers and Sisters in Christ - we cannot save ourselves; Jesus Christ is our Savior. And it's in the next scripture where we find the direct answer to the question:

> *God presented Christ as a sacrifice of atonement, through the shedding of His blood- to be received by faith. He did this to demonstrate His righteousness [which demands punishment for sin], because in His forbearance [deliberate restraint] He had left the sins committed beforehand unpunished – He did it to demonstrate His righteousness at the present time, so as to be just and the one who justifies those who have faith in Jesus.*[60]

This "sacrifice of atonement" refers to reparation for sin. Christ paid our debt by shedding His blood so that we could be forgiven. So, that is how God can be both just and the justifier of sinners.

In God's righteousness, He will punish every sin (Good judge). But in His love, He became a man (So we could be forgiven).

Let's break it down:

To bring about our salvation, God became a man. An actual historical person. He fulfilled prophecies about the promised Messiah that were recorded in the Holy Scriptures centuries before His birth. One of those prophecies was that He would be sinless and would live in accordance with the law of God. This is the law that we have absolutely no chance of perfectly following ourselves. He went on to suffer and died on the cross with a crown of thorns, twisted and placed on his head. But it took more than physical death to accomplish His mission. On the cross, He bared all our sins and shame and was crushed under the Holy wrath of God. The exact measure of wrath needed to satisfy justice was poured out on Him. Upon completion, He said, "It is finished." He didn't say, "I am finished." Meaning He had accomplished His mission and paid our debt in full. He took our place and humbly received the wrath that we deserved. He died — for the "wages of sin is death." [61] But on the third day, He raised Himself from the dead as our risen and victorious Savior.

And by His wounds we are healed:[62]

*He was delivered over to death for our sins and was raised to life for our **justification**.[63]*

Justification means that God declares you legally right with Him. In other words, God has declared that Christ's sacrifice has fully atoned for the sins of the people. Therefore, every one of us can be saved because of the sacrifice of Jesus Christ!

For if, by the trespass of one man, death reigned through that one man, how much more will those who receive God's abundant provision of grace and of the gift of righteousness reign in life through the one man, Jesus Christ! Consequently, just as one trespass resulted in condemnation for all people, so also one righteous act resulted in justification and life for all people. For just as through the disobedience of one man the many were made sinners, so also through the obedience of the one man the many will be made righteous."[64]

Amazing! Jesus Christ is the answer. But this naturally leads to the next question: "What do I need to do to get this forgiveness in my life?" Let's go...

Chapter 8

WHAT MUST I DO TO BE SAVED?

Come to me, all you who are weary and burdened, and I will give you rest. Take my yoke upon you and learn from me, for I am gentle and humble in heart, and you will find rest for your souls. For my yoke is easy and my burden is light.[65]

Jesus demonstrated that He is the Messiah (Christ) by rising up from the dead. He has ascended to heaven, is seated at the right hand of God (The Father)[66], and He will judge the living and the dead.[67] The Bible says that though we have all broken God's law and deserve hell, our sins can be removed from our record!

Come now, and let us reason together, says the Lord. Though your sins are like scarlet, They shall be as white as snow; Though they are red like crimson, They shall be as wool.[68]

So - what exactly does someone need to do to be saved? As usual, we don't need to guess. We can read:

> And they brought them to the magistrates and said, "These men, being Jews, exceedingly trouble our city; and they teach customs which are not lawful for us, being Romans, to receive or observe." Then the multitude rose up together against them; and the magistrates tore off their clothes and commanded them to be beaten with rods. And when they had laid many stripes on them, they threw them into prison, commanding the jailer to keep them securely. Having received such a charge, he put them into the inner prison and fastened their feet in the stocks.[69]

What follows is incredible. After being stripped, beaten, and thrown in jail for no good reason – the Apostle Paul and Silas react by praising God through the night.

> But at midnight Paul and Silas were praying and singing hymns to God, and the prisoners were listening to them.[70]

And, in return, God demonstrated His power.

> Suddenly, there was a great earthquake, so that the foundations of the prison were shaken; and immediately all the doors were opened and everybody's chains were loosed.[71]

When the jailer awoke, he went to take his own life. That would be preferable to what would happen to Roman guards who allowed prisoners in their care to escape.

> *And the keeper of the prison, awakening from sleep and seeing the prison doors open, supposing the prisoners had fled, drew his sword and was about to kill himself. But Paul called with a loud voice saying, "Do yourself no harm, for we are all here."*[72]

And here is the critical moment...

> *Then he (the jailer) called for a light, ran in, and fell down trembling before Paul and Silas. And he brought them out and said,* **"Sirs, what must I do to be saved?"**[73]

"What must I do to be saved?" This question asked 2,000 years ago is the very same question that unbelievers who are presented with the Gospel ask today, and the answer is clear in scripture.

> *So they said,* **"Believe in the Lord Jesus, and you will be saved,"**[74]

Brothers and Sisters in Christ, those we witness to need to understand that they don't need to carry out some heroic performance to be saved. They simply need to believe in Jesus Christ.

But what exactly does that mean? It's crucial we point out that the scripture says we must believe **in** Jesus Christ. There is a difference between believing "in" and believing "that." Many believe *that* God exists or *that*

Jesus, the man, was a wise teacher. But the Bible clearly says this is not what it means to believe...

> *You believe **that** there is one God. Good! Even the demons believe that- and shudder.* [75]

As my Pastor would echo, "Congratulations. You're now on the same level as the devil."

Believing in Jesus Christ requires exclusivity. In other words, there is no backup plan. As it respects our salvation, we must deny our faith in all else - things like our own self-righteousness and religiosity. We must trust in the person and work of Jesus Christ *exclusively*. Certainly, there is no other name by which we can be saved. [76]Jesus did not sacrifice everything on the cross so that He could be one of a multitude of options for salvation. He did not claim to be *a way* to salvation. He said, "I am *the way*, the truth, and the life. No one comes to the Father except through me."[77]

So, no amount of our own good deeds can accomplish our salvation. We know we cannot earn it. The Bible says that, "Clearly no one who relies on the law is justified before God, because 'the righteous will live by faith.'"[78] It is *only* by believing in Jesus that we receive the free gift of salvation:

> *For it is by grace you have been saved, through faith – and this is not from yourselves, it is the gift of God- not by works, so that no one can boast.*[79]

Pastor Paul Washer illustrates this point by inviting students to his hypothetical world religions class. He says you'd love to take this class because it teaches that there are only two religions. It's either Christianity or everything else because Christianity is a religion of grace, and every other religion on Earth is a religion of works. In other words, Christians are justified by their faith in Jesus Christ. It is all about who Jesus is and what He accomplished. There is no self-righteousness in being saved – it's all about Jesus' righteousness. Salvation is a free gift (grace by faith).

In every other religious system, salvation must be "earned" one way or another. As Pastor John MacArthur puts it, "That's hell's answer. The Gospel gives the true answer."

Friend, this is the greatest offer ever made. We can't earn it, can't deserve it, and can't work for it, but we can receive salvation by trusting in Christ alone.

Now - some people will be thinking, "This all sounds great. But you don't know about my past and the things I've done." So we must remind them of perhaps the best-known verse in all of scripture, John 3:16.

> *For God so loved the world that He gave His one and only Son,*
> *that **whoever believes in Him shall not perish but have***
> ***eternal life.***

Whoever believes in Him shall not perish. This is God's promise to *all sinners* – including the worst of sinners. There's a reason it's called the Good News of Jesus Christ! Your sin is not greater than what Jesus accomplished on the cross.

Brothers and Sisters in Christ - this is the Gospel! Let's put it all together and look at the greatest offer in history...

The Gospel - translated Good News, Good Announcement, or Good Message – is the good news about the person and work of Jesus Christ

Starting point: how did we get from "in the beginning, it was very good" to... this?

- You and I are sinful and evil (Original Sin)

- God is separate from everything that is sinful and evil (He is Holy)

- Sin causes a separation from our Creator, which is exactly why so many people believe that "something isn't right about the world and how life is."

- We long for reconciliation with God, and nothing else in this world can fill the "God-shaped hole" in our hearts. We cannot escape the reality that we are sinners who are separated from our Creator.

- Unresolved, an afterlife spent separate from our Creator happens in a place called hell. Jesus preached more about hell than everyone else in the Bible combined.

- The Law is God's standard for acceptance into heaven (The Ten Commandments). Jesus personified the law, so to earn your way into heaven, you have to be as perfect as Jesus Christ, which is impossible.

- We also can't just be pardoned – good judges don't pardon guilty sinners, corrupt judges do.

- This is what the entire Bible is about: how can God be a good judge and also forgive guilty sinners (us!)?

- The answer is Jesus. In God's righteousness, He will punish every sin (good judge), but in His love, He became a Man (so we can be forgiven). Jesus then bore our sin on that cross and said, "It is finished," when He had done what was required to satisfy God's justice against the people.

- To obtain this forgiveness and be saved, we must abandon every backup plan and believe in Jesus Christ alone for salvation. Jesus is the way, the truth, and the life. No one comes to the Father except through Him.

- God so loved the world that He gave His only son, that **whoever believes** in Him will not perish but have eternal life. That means this Gospel is God's promise to ALL sinners. Nothing you have done is bigger than what Jesus accomplished on the cross.

Want to keep these points on hand and share them with your brothers and sisters in Christ? Click HERE or visit authorjamesfinke.com/freeres ources for a downloadable, printable, shareable infographic!

This Gospel is the power of God.[80] It is the greatest offer in history, and we have a direct command from Jesus Christ to share it with all nations. We must expect follow-up questions from the people we witness to. Especially, "How do I know if it 'worked'?" Let's address some of the most common Gospel questions out there...

PART 2 – FAQ'S

Chapter 9

HOW DO I KNOW IF I'M ACTUALLY SAVED?

I f you have accepted Jesus Christ as your Lord and personal Savior, then you should receive your official certificate of completion in the mail within 6-8 weeks.

Just kidding.

The greatest indicator that you've been saved is the existence of *sanctification* in your life, which refers to the <u>process</u> of becoming holy.

> *Continually pursue peace with everyone, and the sanctification without which no one will [ever] see the Lord.* -Hebrews 12:14

This is critical to understand the difference between justification and sanctification. Justification (being saved and declared legally right with God) happens immediately when we believe. But sanctification (becoming holy) is a process that occurs over a lifetime. The Bible teaches that "*He who has begun a good work in you will complete it...*"[81]

Remember – to be holy means to be *separate* from that which is sinful and evil. Sanctification also describes the process of becoming more like

Jesus and less like our sinful world. Therefore, if you claim to have accepted Jesus Christ and absolutely nothing else changes in your life, what would make you believe you've actually been converted?

Pastor Voddie Baucham explains it this way: God will change your "want to." What it means is that you'll have new desires, and you'll live differently from the sinful world. This describes how *repentance* goes hand in hand with believing *in* Jesus for salvation. To repent means to turn away from our sins and to God. Believing in Jesus means that you're turned away from sin for salvation. It's an eagerness to be righteous and to abandon all unrighteousness. The Bible teaches that God *grants* repentance to those who have believed and not those who earned it. We can't clean up our lives to be good enough to enter the kingdom of God. Thus, repentance is part of the saving work that *God does* in the heart.[82]

Let's read how God describes the process of being taken out of the world and made holy:

> *For I will take you out of the nations; I will gather you from all the countries and bring you back into your own land. I will sprinkle clean water on you, and you will be made clean; I will cleanse you from all your impurities and from all your idols. I will give you a new heart and put a new spirit in you; I will remove from you your heart of stone and give you a heart of flesh. And I will put my Spirit in you and move you to follow my decrees and be careful to keep my laws.* [83]

Does that mean you're immediately a perfect person?

No – you will continue to sin, but God will not let you get away with it. You won't be able to stand it when you sin because the Holy Spirit will discipline you. Even in your mistakes, it will be evident that you are growing in holiness. My Pastor compares this to the "rumble strips" we find on the edge of the highway. Just as those rumble strips give you an immediate and jarring warning every time you veer off course, the Holy Spirit will do the same.

And is it any surprise? Those who are saved are children of God. Am I to believe our Heavenly Father is a deadbeat Dad? Of course not. He will be involved in His children's lives, including sanctification. The Bible tells us as much:

> *Endure hardship as discipline; God is treating you as His chil-*
> *dren. For what children are not disciplined by their Father?*
> *If you are not disciplined- and everyone undergoes discipline-*
> *then you are not legitimate, not true sons and daughters at all.*
> *Moreover, we have all had human fathers who disciplined us*
> *and we respected them for it. How much more should we submit*
> *to the Father of spirits and live! They disciplined us for a little*
> *while as they thought best; but God disciplines us for our good,*
> *in order that we may share in His holiness. No discipline seems*
> *pleasant at the time, but painful. Later on, however, it produces*
> *a harvest of righteousness for those who have been trained by*
> *it.*[84]

Earlier today, my children were swimming in the pool at the hotel we are staying at. My son and a couple of other kids he met there began to do "cannon balls" as young kids do. They had no nefarious intent, but they were jumping too close to and splashing other guests trying to lounge in the pool. Naturally, I intervened, but my concern was not with the other kids. That's for their parents to do because they are not my concern. I corrected only my son because I love him and I want the best for him. Likewise, our heavenly Father will correct His children because He loves us and wants the best for us.

A parent also corrects their children because it's the parents' reputation that is on the line. For better or worse, a child's behavior is a reflection of his parents. When someone calls themselves a Christian but lives just like the sinful world, they abuse the holy name of Jesus Christ. God is not praised because of them; His name is abused.

Not everyone who calls themselves a Christian is saved. A lot of people are out partying until late hours of the night on Saturday and then wake up hungover to stumble into church on Sunday. So then, if you still act like the world, dress like the world, talk like the world, idolize godless celebrities, and live otherwise just as you used to – it's evidence that you have not actually believed. And God will rectify the situation:

> *And wherever they went among the nations they profaned my holy name, for it was said of them, "These are the Lord's people, and yet they had to leave his land." I had concern for my holy name, which the people of Israel profaned among the nations where they had gone. Therefore, say to the Israelites, "This is what the Sovereign Lord says: It is not for your sake, people of Israel, that I am going to do these things, but for the sake of my holy name, which you have profaned among the nations where you have gone. I will show the holiness of my great name which has been profaned among the nations, the name you have profaned among them. Then the nations will know that I am the Lord, declares the Sovereign Lord, when I am proved holy through you before their eyes."*[85]

God will be proven Holy through His children. Every Christian is a demonstration of God's power. Hence, if you've been saved, those who knew you in the past will marvel because you will continue to change. That's true for everyone, whether it's someone who was supposedly righteous or for an inmate in a supermax prison. It's also true for the former alcoholic and for the former atheist. God will change their "want to" and will sanctify them. As Jesus said, you will "know them by their fruit." [86]

Chapter 10

WHY IS BEING SAVED SOMETIMES REFERRED TO AS BEING "BORN AGAIN"?

The term "born again" comes from one of the best-known passages in all of scripture. Let's read:

Jesus Teaches Nicodemus

*Now there was a Pharisee, a man named Nicodemus who was a member of the Jewish ruling council. He came to Jesus at night and said, "Rabbi, we know that you are a teacher who has come from God. For no one could perform the signs you are doing if God were not with him." Jesus replied, **"Very truly I tell you, no one can see the kingdom of God unless they are born again**." "How can someone be born when they are old?"*

Nicodemus asked. "Surely they cannot enter a second time into their mother's womb to be born!" Jesus answered, "Very truly I tell you, no one can enter the kingdom of God unless they are born of water and the Spirit. Flesh gives birth to flesh, but the Spirit gives birth to spirit. You should not be surprised at my saying, 'You must be born again.' The wind blows wherever it pleases. You hear its sound, but you cannot tell where it comes from or where it is going. So it is with everyone born of the Spirit." "How can this be?" Nicodemus asked. "You are Israel's teacher," said Jesus, "and do you not understand these things? Very truly I tell you, we speak of what we know, and we testify to what we have seen, but still you people do not accept our testimony. I have spoken to you of earthly things and you do not believe; how then will you believe if I speak of heavenly things? No one has ever gone into heaven except the one who came from heaven—the Son of Man. Just as Moses lifted up the snake in the wilderness, so the Son of Man must be lifted up, that everyone who believes may have eternal life in him." For God so loved the world that he gave his one and only Son, that whoever believes in him shall not perish but have eternal life. For God did not send his Son into the world to condemn the world, but to save the world through him. Whoever believes in him is not condemned, but whoever does not believe stands condemned already because they have not believed in the name of God's one and only Son."[87]

This incredible passage deserves its own book, but for our purposes, let's hit some of the key points. Jesus teaches an elite religious leader that, in order to be saved, we must be reborn spiritually. This is known as the doctrine of "regeneration." The wages of sin is death, but the gift of God is eternal life.[88]

Our "birth from above" means that the true believer is literally a new creation (spiritually).

> *Therefore, if anyone is in Christ, he is a new creation. The old has passed away; behold, the new has come.*[89]

This ties right in with the sanctification (the process of becoming holy) we discussed earlier in Chapter 9. The believer isn't perfect, but their life will have taken a dramatic change in direction. They will desire to practice righteousness **because they are a new creation in Christ**. "*For we are His workmanship, created in Christ Jesus for good works...*" [90] Will believers still sin? Of course, because we're still fallen. But we will continue to become more like Jesus and less like the sin-filled world.

Now- there is another major takeaway from this passage, one that we can *all* relate to. It has to do with our birth. Imagine receiving a special award for your birth. You were nominated, a committee reviewed your past, and ultimately you were chosen for the award. Your friends and family gushed over your momentous achievement, and you're asked to give an acceptance speech.

That would be a bizarre and absurd scenario *because we have no part to play in our own birth*. It's no personal accomplishment that deserves an award.

And that, my friend, is what Jesus is explaining to Nicodemus. **Being born again is not a personal accomplishment**. Only God can transform us spiritually. "*He chose to give us birth through the word of truth, that we might be a kind of first fruits of all He created.*"[91] This "word of truth" is the Gospel! So, we know that we can only receive salvation through

God's grace and faith in Jesus Christ alone. This separates Christianity from every other religion, and it leaves those honestly seeking God with a very reasonable question:

If there is nothing I can do to earn salvation... what *can* I do?

This is a great mystery of the Gospel. And the wisest counsel I've heard[92] is simply this:

Ask.

Ask God that, in His mercy and grace, He would open your eyes. Deny yourselves and follow God, surrender all to Him, and believe in Jesus Christ alone. He's already told you to:

> *Ask and it will be given to you, seek and you will find, knock and the door will be opened to you. For everyone who asks receives; the one who seeks finds; and to the one who knocks, the door will be opened.*[93]

Chapter 11

DO YOU NEED TO BE BAPTIZED TO BE SAVED?

I n short – no. Salvation is a free gift from God (grace) when we believe in Christ alone. Baptism is not an added "requirement." However, if you've been saved, you're called to be baptized. Let's look into the message of the cross to understand:

> *Two other men, both criminals, were also led out with him to be executed. When they came to the place called the skull, they crucified Him there, along with the criminals – one on His right, the other on His left... One of the criminals who hung there hurled insults at him: "Aren't you the Messiah? Save yourself and us!" But the other criminal rebuked him. "Don't you fear God," he said, "since you are under the same sentence? We are punished justly, for we are getting what our deeds deserve. But this man has done nothing wrong." Then he said, "Jesus, remember me when you come into your kingdom."*

Jesus answered him, "Truly I tell you, today you will be with me in paradise."[94]

This incredible passage of the criminal being saved on the cross buttresses the point. Obviously, the criminal was not baptized, yet he was saved by belief in Jesus.

So, if baptism isn't required to be saved, how does it relate to salvation?

Baptism is to salvation, as a wedding ring is to marriage.

In other words, it's a public demonstration of your commitment. The wedding ring does not *cause* you to love your spouse, but you wear it as a public testimony that you are married. Likewise, baptism does not save you, but you do it as a public testimony that you've been converted.

It's a symbol of our commitment. We know God teaches spiritual concepts using symbols, parables, analogies, etc. Being immersed in water and brought out again symbolizes being born again. It demonstrates the death and burial of our old self and our re-birth (regeneration) as a new creation. Specifically, as a new creation that has been cleansed from sin and justified in the eyes of the Lord.

The Bible teaches that our old self is crucified, buried, and resurrected with Christ when we are saved.

"Or don't you know that all of us who were baptized into Christ Jesus were baptized into his death? We were therefore buried with him through baptism into death in order that, just as Christ was raised from the dead through the glory of the Father,

we too may live a new life. For if we have been united with
him in a death like his, we will certainly also be united with
him in a resurrection like his. For we know that our old self was
crucified with him so that the body ruled by sin might be done
away with, that we should no longer be slaves to sin—because
anyone who has died has been set free from sin."[95]

Now, some may ask: if baptism is just a symbol, isn't it enough if I believe in my heart that I've been converted? But that viewpoint misses a critical element of baptism: **it is a direct command from our Lord Jesus Christ to do it.**

Jesus commanded His followers to "Go and make disciples of all nations, baptizing them in the name of the Father, and of the Son, and of the Holy Spirit." So, to be baptized is to be obedient to the command of Jesus, which means it's a "no-brainer" for all Christians!

Next comes the question, when should someone be baptized? Scripture clearly says that we ought to be baptized as soon as we're saved. To illustrate this, let's return to the jailer who got saved after the prison doors flew open and Paul and Silas' chains were loosed.

The jailer called for lights, rushed in and fell trembling before
Paul and Silas. He then brought them out and asked, "Sirs,
what must I do to be saved? They replied, "Believe in the Lord
Jesus, and you will be saved- you and your household." Then
they spoke the word of the Lord to him and to all the others in
*his house. **At that hour of the night the jailer took them***
and washed their wounds, then immediately he and all
his household were baptized.[96]

The entire family was saved and got baptized *in the middle of the night*. They didn't throw out a bunch of proposed dates and then wait to see which worked best for the group. They didn't even go to sleep and then head down to the river after breakfast the next day. They were saved, and then they were immediately baptized. We see the same incidence when Peter preached on the day of Pentecost.

Those who accepted his message were baptized, and about three thousand were added to their number that day.[97]

Three thousand people were saved and likewise 3,000 people were baptized. The urgency and consistency with which we see these baptisms in the Bible should be instructive to believers, regardless of how long they've been saved. If you've not been baptized, the time to do it is now.

Pastor John MacArthur has pointed out an interesting paradox related to baptism. For various reasons, many born-again believers in Christ have never been baptized. Likewise, countless people have been baptized (normally as infants) and have absolutely nothing to do with Christ or the church. So, you have unbaptized believers and baptized unbelievers. Neither is good.

It should also be noted that there is a significant disagreement amongst Christians on the issue of baptism. Some churches teach infant baptism, while others teach a "believer's baptism" that occurs after someone has been saved. Some baptisms involve a "sprinkling" or pouring over of water, while others involve a complete immersion. However, it is important to point out that issues like church governance, style of worship, and baptism, while important, are not salvation issues. Disagreement on secondary issues is different than disagreement on major Christian doctrines such as the trinity, the authority of scripture, the deity of Jesus, etc.

It's not uncommon to hear objections from unbelievers that say something to the effect of: "Christianity can't be true. You guys don't even agree on what is correct within the faith." In these situations, I find it helpful to point out that there is massive disagreement among scientists on various issues, such as evolution. We can ask them if they believe that there is still some truth about our universe despite obvious disagreements. Of course, there is. Likewise, there is still spiritual truth we can know despite disagreement amongst Christians.

To wrap up this issue, I will share with you that I was baptized as an infant. However, as you can probably tell from this chapter, it is my personal conviction that the Bible teaches a "believer's baptism" involving complete immersion in water. This photo captures the glorious day that my family and I were baptized as born-again believers in the Lord Jesus Christ.

Chapter 12

ISN'T IT CLOSE-MINDED AND INTOLERANT TO BELIEVE JESUS IS THE ONLY WAY TO BE SAVED?

To all those who believe that there are no "absolutes" in life, the absolute exclusivity of the Gospel is scandalous. To all those who advocate living "your truth," the definitive claim that Jesus is *the truth* is offensive. And to all those who subscribe to a pluralistic worldview, it may sound closed-minded and downright antagonistic to claim that Jesus Christ is the only way to heaven.

Yet that is precisely what the Gospel earnestly proclaims.

Pastor Paul Washer illustrates this sentiment when he says that millions of Americans would instantly change their views on Christianity if we would just change one word. And that word is "the." If Christians would proclaim that Jesus is *"a" Savior* instead of *"the"* Savior, they would accept it. Yet Christians tirelessly claim that Jesus is *the only way.*

Why?

Let's break it down.

First, we must point out that this isn't the decision of Christians. Jesus Christ said, "I am the way, the truth, and the life."[98] Notice he did not claim to be "a way, a truth, or a life." And in case there was any room for ambiguity, the very next thing He said was, "No one comes to the Father except through me."[99] Case closed.

Jesus Christ taught that He is the only path to salvation. That is why, immediately following His resurrection, His Apostles taught the same. When Peter addressed the Sanhedrin (Ruling Council of the Jews), He told them:

> *Then Peter, filled with the Holy Spirit, said to them, "Rulers of the people and elders of Israel: If we this day are judged for a good deed done to a helpless man, by what means he has been made well, let it be known to you all, and to all the people of Israel, that by the name of Jesus Christ of Nazareth, whom you crucified, whom God raised from the dead, by Him this man stands here before you whole. This is the 'stone which was rejected by you builders, which has become the chief cornerstone.' Nor is there salvation in any other, for there is no other name under heaven given among men by which we must be saved.*[100]

The second important point to note is that this is not some arbitrary decision from Jesus. This is why Christians must have a firm grasp on exactly what the Gospel teaches. In the light of the true Gospel, sinners can understand that Jesus is the only way to heaven because He is the sole remedy to sin. Only Jesus was qualified to bear our sins and be punished in our place to satisfy God's righteous anger. "God so loved the world that He gave His only Son, that whoever believes in Him shall not perish but have eternal life." And people honestly believe that Jesus came, suffered, was crucified, and died to be one of the myriads of options for our salvation? I don't think so.

Thirdly, Christians won't budge on the exclusivity of the Gospel because it's not ours to change! RC Sproul explains that when the Bible refers to "The Gospel of God" in Romans 1, it doesn't simply mean it's a Gospel *about God* but the structure of the sentence in the original Greek is such that it means the Gospel *belongs to God*. Yes, Paul is describing an announcement that is *owned* by God. So, to try to change it to meet your personal tastes and preferences means you are attempting to (and failing) improve that which is authored by the Creator of the universe Himself.

Yet, false teachers have attempted to do this virtually since the Gospel was delivered. They pervert the message typically by preaching Christ "plus" something else. The Bible's response is once again swift and clear:

> *I marvel that you are turning away so soon from Him who called you in the grace of Christ, to a different gospel, which is not another; but there are some who trouble you and want to pervert the gospel of Christ. But even if we, or an angel from heaven, preach any other gospel to you than what we have preached to you, let him be accursed. As we have said before, so now I say again, if anyone preaches any other gospel to you than what you have received, let him be accursed.*[101]

Remember how we discussed that this form of repetition is used sparingly in the Bible and only for points that the author is hammering home? Well, here is another example. Therefore, if someone preaches to you another gospel, let them be accursed.

So, it's not arrogant to claim that Jesus is the only way. On the contrary, it's obedient. And we know Christians are the only people who can say they are going to heaven without boasting or being self-righteous. Because every other religion requires "earning" your way to heaven through works. Only Christianity is a religion of grace where heaven cannot be earned.

As for the charge of being narrow-minded, I would point to a brilliant example I heard from Lee Strobel (former atheist and author of "Case for Christ.") He told a story of a couple who had a baby diagnosed with jaundice. Most of us know that, while jaundice is a serious liver issue, it is quite easily solved by placing the baby under a special light to stimulate the liver.

Now, the parents could object to this treatment, and they could try scrubbing the baby with soap or dipping her in bleach to fix her coloring. And the doctor would say, "No, no, no. There is only one way to cure this condition, and that is by placing her under the light." But the parents could choose to ignore the problem and live "their truth." They could sincerely believe that the baby would just be fine on her own.

But they would be sincerely wrong.

The doctor could point out that she has been in practice for 30+ years and is an expert in this field. She could also tell the parents to trust her because she has cured countless other patients of this condition.

Now, would anybody accuse the parents of being narrow-minded if they trusted that doctor to pursue the only course of treatment?

Of course not. It's not narrow-minded to act rationally based on the evidence. And the evidence says that Jesus is exactly who He says He is.

What evidence? I'm glad you asked. That's next...

Chapter 13

HOW DO WE KNOW JESUS IS WHO HE SAID HE IS?

There is another book in this series, Jesus: Fib, Dead, or God? that is dedicated to answering the most important question asked by the most important person in history. The person is Jesus of Nazareth, and the question is, "Who do you say that I am?" It would be outside the scope of this book to go through it all, but let's hit some key points as they pertain to the Gospel.

To start, we recognize that virtually all views of Jesus fall into one of three categories.

1. *Fib-* Jesus, the man, never existed

2. *Dead-* Jesus, the man, existed, but He was just a guy and is, therefore, now dead.

3. *God-* Jesus is exactly who He said He is.

We immediately dismiss *Fib* because it's an outright silly theory. Even other atheist scholars cringe when people claim that Jesus, the man, never existed. It is a non-issue for historians of antiquity. So, those who claim Jesus never existed instantly lose any credibility since it's not consistent with the facts.

This leaves us with *Dead* or *God*. In other words, was He just a guy? Or something more?

The answer to this issue lies in an actual historical event: the resurrection. If Jesus rose from the dead, Christianity is true. And the Bible pushes the chips to the middle of the table on this issue:

> *And if Christ has not been raised, your faith is futile; you are still in your sins.*[102]

So, how do we examine the claim that the resurrection is an actual historical event? There are many ways to do it, but I particularly like the "Minimal Facts Argument" from Dr. Gary Habermas when dealing with new believers or unbelievers. Again, "Jesus: Fib, Dead, or God?" breaks this down in detail, but here is the gist:

The minimal facts approach uses only evidence considered undeniable, even to skeptics. To qualify, the evidence (1) must be confirmed by several strong and independent sources, and (2) must be recognized as historical by the vast majority of scholars specializing in a relevant field of study. This includes liberal and even atheist specialist scholars. The sources come from the Bible but also from numerous non-Biblical sources – including sources that are hostile to Christianity. Here are 5 of these undeniable historical facts.

F.A.C.T.S.

- F- Final Breath - Jesus died by crucifixion.

- A - Appearances. Soon after, His followers had real experiences that they believed were appearances from the risen Jesus.

- C- Change - as in radical change. His followers' lives were transformed due to these appearances, to the point that they were willing to die specifically for their faith in the resurrection.

- T- Taught- these things were taught very soon after the resurrection. They proclaimed Jesus as the Messiah, the Son of the Living God.

- S- Skeptics- Some of the most unlikely people were converted, including Saul of Tarsus (Paul) and James, the brother of Jesus, who thought Jesus was insane when He went to the cross.

When we consider this fact pattern, we realize that Jesus was telling the truth. He is the Messiah, the Son of the Living God. In other words, I choose to believe Jesus rose from the dead due to F.A.C.T.S.

The bottom line is that Jesus rose from the dead, proving He is God the Son.

To corroborate this reality, you can point out that Jesus did these things in fulfillment of specific prophecies. God promised the nation of Israel that He would provide them a Deliverer. This Deliverer is known as the Messiah, or "anointed one." The Old Testament scriptures are loaded with specific prophecies about this Messiah. Here are a few that were recorded centuries before Jesus was born:

- He will be born of a virgin- Isaiah 7:14

- He will be born in a tiny town called Bethlehem- Micah 5:2

- He will be a miracle worker- Isaiah 35:5

- He will be executed among sinners- Isaiah 53:12

- He will pray for His persecutors- Isaiah 53:12

- He will have His hands and feet pierced- Psalm 22:16

- He will be raised from the dead and seated at the right hand of God- Psalm 110:1

These are just a handful of prophecies. Indeed it is incredible. To help convince unbelievers, I encourage them to read Isaiah 53. When they finish it and agree that the passage is about Jesus, then I will indicate that it was recorded 700 years before Jesus's birth. Men can't predict the future, but it seems that the author of the Bible can.

So, we know that (1) the evidence indicates that Jesus rose from the dead and (2) these things were done in fulfillment of specific prophecies. To put a bow on the issue, I suggest (3) pointing out the radical transformation of people who put their faith in Jesus. Almost everyone knows someone whose life dramatically changed direction as a result of finding Jesus. Other religious leaders have claimed to hear from God, but Jesus claimed to BE God. Today, ~2,000 years after His death, billions worship this first-century carpenter. "I am far within the mark when I say that all the armies that ever marched, all the navies that were ever built; all the parliaments that ever sat and all the kings that ever reigned, put together, have not affected the life of man upon this earth as powerfully as that one solitary life." [103]

Chapter 14

WHY ARE THERE 4 GOSPELS IN THE BIBLE?

The Gospel is the good news about the person and work of Jesus Christ. So, why are there four gospels in the Bible?

In short, they're all telling the same story but from different perspectives. So let's break them down in the order they appear in the Bible.

1. *The Gospel According to Matthew*- Matthew was a Jewish man who wrote to a Jewish audience, convincing them that Jesus is the promised Messiah. The primary purpose of his gospel was to demonstrate that God has kept His ancient promises to Israel. That's why, for instance, his gospel opens with the genealogy of Jesus. Matthew is showing that Jesus is in the line of David, Israel's most famous king, and Abraham, Israel's founding patriarch.[1] Matthew knew that his audience believed in the authority of the Old Testament Scriptures, so he utilized them as evidence that Jesus was the promised Messiah. Here are a handful of examples:

Matthew quotes the prophet Isaiah, who foretold that the Messiah would be born of a virgin:

All of this took place to fulfill what the Lord had said through the prophet: "The virgin will conceive and give birth to a son, and they will call him Immanuel (which means 'God with us')."[105]

Matthew quotes the prophet Isaiah, who foretold that the Messiah would be a miracle-working healer.

When evening came, many who were demon-possessed were brought to Him, and He drove out the spirits with a word and healed all the sick. This was to fulfill what was spoken through the prophet Isaiah: "He took up our infirmities and bore our diseases."[106]

Matthew also quotes the prophet Micah, who prophesied that the Messiah would be born in the little town of Bethlehem.

When King Herod heard this he was disturbed, and all of Jerusalem with him. When he had called together all the people's chief priests and teachers of the law, he asked them where the Messiah was to be born. In Bethlehem in Judea, they replied, for this is what the prophet has written: "But you, Bethlehem, in the land of Judah, are by no means among the rulers of Judah; for our of you will come a ruler who will shepherd my people Israel.[107]

Matthew quotes the psalmist, who foretold that the Messiah would teach using parables:

Jesus spoke all these things to the crowd in parables; he did not say anything to them without using a parable. So it was fulfilled what was spoken through the prophet: "I will open my mouth in parables, I will utter things hidden since the creation of the world."[108]

2. The Gospel According to Mark- Mark was a Jewish man writing to a Roman audience. Therefore, he focused more on what Jesus did than what Jesus said. He did not emphasize Old Testament scripture references or include things like the genealogy as they would be of less interest to a Roman reader. The hallmark of Mark's gospel is its brevity. It is the shortest of the Gospels and is action-packed. Mark consistently uses "immediately" and "straightaway." He focused on what a Roman reader would be most captivated by – miracles, healings, control over nature, etc. In the first chapter alone, Mark records Jesus (1) casting out an unclean spirit, (2) healing Peter's mother of a fever, (3) healing many diseases and casting out demons, and (4) cleansing a leper. That's in one chapter! Of course, Mark goes on to tell of Jesus calming storms, feeding thousands, and walking on water, among many other miracles.

3. The Gospel According to Luke- Luke was not an eyewitness. He doesn't claim to be. Rather, he is a historian who claims to have traced the info from eyewitnesses. Chief among his witnesses was the apostle Peter and Mary, the mother of Jesus. Luke's goal is to write an orderly account. He is focused on history and chronology. Also of note is that Luke is the only gentile (non-Jewish) writer of a Gospel. He is focused on reaching a gentile audience, highlighting Jesus' love for gentiles. This includes groups considered outcasts like lepers, prostitutes, tax collectors, sinners, and Samaritans. For example, in Luke 7 we read about the prostitute who washed Jesus' feet with her tears. This story is not recorded in any of the other gospels.

4. The Gospel According to John- The Apostle John wrote his gospel with the clear goal of evangelism. He is writing to everyone. *And truly Jesus did many other signs in the presence of His disciples, which are not written in this book; but these are written that you may believe that Jesus is the Christ, the Son of God, and that believing you may have life in His name.*[109] John's gospel is believed to have been the last of the four recorded. It is not simply a restating of what was already recorded, as 93% of its content is not found in the other gospels. Notably, John's gospel includes seven statements that Jesus made about Himself. The seven "I am" statements:

1.   I Am the Bread of Life- John 6
2.   I Am the Light of the World- John 8
3.   I Am the Door- John 10
4.   I Am the Good Shepherd- John 10
5.   I Am the Resurrection and the Life- John 11
6.   I Am the Way, the Truth, and the Life- John 14
7.   I Am the True Vine- John 15

Now – it's not uncommon to hear skeptics claim that the Gospels contradict one another. This should not surprise us since undermining the word of God is (literally) the devil's oldest trick in the book. The enemy has been doing it since the Garden of Eden when he deceived Adam and Eve with, "Did God *really* say you can't eat from the tree?" Combine that with sinners who are desperate to justify their unbelief, and you get objections like this:

"Matthew says that there was one angel at the tomb. But Luke says that there are two angels at the tomb. Those statements contradict. Those statements are..."

Actually, those statements are exactly what you'd expect of actual eye-witness evidence. Investigative experts will tell you that the very nature of eyewitness testimony is agreement on the major event and divergent secondary details. If every single secondary detail was exactly the same, it would indicate collusion. Beyond that, the statements don't even actually contradict. Matthew doesn't say there is *only* one. He simply mentions one, and there are many reasons why that may have been the case. Finally – and this is just common sense – if there were actually contradictions in the Bible that could falsify it, it would have been done long ago. The Bible is, by far, the most scrutinized book in history, and it's not close.

This is just one example of the countless attacks against the Bible and, therefore, the Gospel. It would be outside the scope of this project to go through them all, but another book in this series, The Bible Uncomplicated, does a deep dive on these issues. For our purposes here, it's important we recognize that we have four gospels that complement one another, not contradict. It's one story told from four different perspectives.

70	Matthew	Mark	Luke	John
Portrait of Jesus	King	Servant	Man	God
Original Readers	Jews	Romans	Gentiles	Everyone
Key Features	Sermons	Miracles	Parables	Teachings

Chapter 15

WHAT ABOUT THE OLD TESTAMENT OF THE BIBLE?

There is a common misconception about the Bible that the New Testament is about Jesus and the Old Testament is about everything else. This belief means that the Gospel is exclusively a "New Testament thing." But that is simply not true. The reality is that Jesus Christ is the main theme *of the entire Bible.* As Pastor Steve Lawson eloquently summed it up, "The Old Testament says He's coming, The New Testament says He's here, The Book of Acts proclaims Him, the epistles explain Him, and Revelation says He's coming again." It's all about Jesus.

To support this, we can go right to the words of our Lord Jesus, Himself. The Gospel of Luke records an amazing situation that occurred on the very day Jesus rose from the dead. He appeared to two of His disciples on the road to Emmaus and gave them a master class on... Him!

> Then He said to them, "O foolish ones, and slow of heart to
> believe in all that the prophets have spoken! Ought not the

Christ to have suffered these things and to enter His glory?"
And beginning at Moses and all the Prophets, He expounded
to them in all the Scriptures the things concerning Himself.[110]

Jesus subsequently appeared to his Apostles and "opened their understanding" so that they, too, could comprehend how the scriptures were about Him. Keep in mind that the only scriptures written at this time were the Old Testament scriptures.

And He opened their understanding that they might compre-
hend the scriptures. Then He said to them, "Thus it is written,
and thus it was necessary for the Christ to suffer and to rise
from the dead the third day, and that repentance and remis-
sion of sins should be preached in His name to all nations,
beginning at Jerusalem. And you are witnesses of these things."
-Luke 24: 45-48

With this understanding, the Apostles used the Old Testament scriptures to preach the Gospel. Paul introduces the gospel as *"the gospel of God which He promised before through His prophets in the Holy scriptures..."*[111] Likewise, Peter's sermon on the day of Pentecost is also built on Old Testament Scriptures.[112] He explained that Jesus is Christ and Lord by quoting from the Prophet Joel and the Prophet (King) David. Upon hearing the preaching, three thousand were saved on that single day.

Jesus explained to His Apostles that His death and resurrection were *always* God's plan for the salvation of the world. Amazingly, we can go back to the very first book in the Bible (the days of the Garden of Eden), and we already see the Gospel being foreshadowed. Look at what God says to the serpent after he deceives Adam and Eve:

> *So the Lord God said to the serpent: Because you have done this, You are cursed more than all cattle, And more than every beat of the field; On your belly you shall go, and you shall eat dust All the days of your life,* ***And I will put enmity Between you and the woman, And between your offspring and hers; He will crush your head And you will bruise His heel.***[113]

This is known as the "Protoevangelium" or "first gospel." It shows that, even from the beginning of time, God had this plan for the salvation of the world. It foreshadows the offspring of the woman (Jesus) who would come to crush the head of the enemy (Satan). As part of that process, He will suffer on the cross (the enemy will "bruise his heel.")

To conclude, I leave you with an Old Testament prophecy that Jesus Himself quoted while on the cross. At three in the afternoon, Jesus cried out, *"My God, my God, why have you forsaken me?"* Let's read the prophecy He was referring to while keeping in mind that this was recorded centuries before Jesus was even born.

> ***My God, my God, why have you forsaken me?*** *Why are you so far from saving me, so far from the words of my groaning? O my God, I cry out by day, but you do not answer, by night, and am not silent. Yet you are enthroned as the Holy One; you are the praise of Israel. In you our fathers put their trust; they trusted and you delivered them. They cried to you*

and were saved; in you they trusted and were not disappointed. But I am a worm and not a man, scorned by men and despised by the people. All who see me mock me; they hurl insults, shaking their heads: "He trusts in the LORD; let the LORD rescue him. Let him deliver him, since he delights in him." Yet you brought me out of the womb; you made me trust in you even at my mother's breast. From birth I was cast upon you; from my mother's womb you have been my God. Do not be far from me, for trouble is near and there is no one to help. Many bulls surround me; strong bulls of Bashan encircle me. Roaring lions tearing their prey open their mouths wide against me. I am poured out like water, and all my bones are out of joint. My heart has turned to wax; it has melted away within me. My strength is dried up like a potsherd, and my tongue sticks to the roof of my mouth; you lay me in the dust of death. Dogs have surrounded me; a band of evil men has encircled me, they have pierced my hands and my feet. I can count all my bones; people stare and gloat over me. They divide my garments among them and cast lots for my clothing. But you, O LORD, be not far off; O my Strength, come quickly to help me. Deliver my life from the sword, my precious life from the power of the dogs. Rescue me from the mouth of the lions; save me from the horns of the wild oxen. I will declare your name to my brothers; in the congregation I will praise you. You who fear the LORD, praise him! All you descendants of Jacob, honor him! Revere him, all you descendants of Israel! For he has not despised or disdained the suffering of the afflicted one; he has not hidden his face from him but has listened to his cry for help. From you comes the theme of my praise in the great assembly; before those who fear you will I fulfill my vows. The poor will eat and be satisfied; they who seek the LORD will praise him-- may your hearts live forever! All the ends of the earth will remember and turn to the LORD, and all the families of the nations will bow down before him, for dominion belongs to the LORD and he rules over the nations. All the rich of the earth will feast and worship; all who go down to the dust will kneel before him-- those who cannot keep themselves alive. Posterity will serve him; future generations will be told about the Lord. They will proclaim his righteousness to a people yet unborn-- for he has done it.[114]

Chapter 16

YOU REALLY BELIEVE THE BIBLE WAS WRITTEN BY GOD?

The Gospel is rooted in the reality that the Bible is indeed the inspired, authoritative word of God. Therefore, when we proclaim the Gospel, we should expect questions about and objections to the authority of the text.

No problem.

Another book in this series, The Bible Uncomplicated, provides a complete business case for why we believe the Bible is true. I highly recommend that volume for a deeper understanding of the subject, but we will also hit some high-level points here as it relates to our topic at hand. In short, sharing the Gospel does not require you to be a Biblical scholar, but it certainly strengthens your case to explain why we believe.

To begin, we need first to define what we mean when we say that God is the author of the Bible. The Bible says that all Scripture is "God-breathed." What does that mean? It does not mean we believe God literally took pen to paper and wrote it down. Of course, He could have, seeing as He created the entire universe from nothing. But that's not what we believe. Nor do we believe that God dictated the words and that the 40+ human writers acted as robotic stenographers. No. Instead, we look at 2 Peter 3: 19-21.

> *We also have the prophetic message as something completely reliable, and you will do well to pay attention to it, as to a light shining in a dark place, until the day dawns and the morning rises in your hearts. Above all, you must understand that no prophecy of Scripture came about by the prophet's own interpretation of things. For prophecy never had its origin in the human will, but prophets, though humans, spoke from God as they were carried along by the Holy Spirit.*

And there we have it. This is what we mean when we say that God is the author of the Bible: God inspired men to write down exactly what He wanted them to, without violating their personalities. [115]

With this established, let's address why we believe it's true.

Our first reason? **Because Jesus says so.** It's that simple. Jesus Christ demonstrated that He is exactly who He said He is by raising from the dead. Therefore, when He says that the Bible is the authoritative word of God, I take that to the bank. He taught that the Bible is inerrant (cannot be mistaken), inspired by the Holy Spirit, timeless, and historically accurate. He even stated that the Bible is more important than physical sustenance. And we believe Him.

We can also support Biblical authority by appealing to various characteristics of the Bible. In "The Bible Uncomplicated," we explain why the Bible is **CORRECT**.

C- Collection - the Bible is different from many holy books because it's a collection of sixty–six books, to be specific.

O- Out in front of science - the author of the Bible is the ultimate expert on how the universe works. We've found out that as science progresses, we can trace discoveries to Bible scriptures written thousands of years prior.

R- Resilient - the Bible is by far the most scrutinized book in history, and yet it still stands.

R- Revered - the authority of the Bible is positioned "above the fold" in all statements of belief of respected Christian churches and ministry organizations.

E- Eyewitness - evidence for the Gospel includes (1) direct evidence in the form of multiple eyewitness accounts from Apostles, (2) an orderly account composed by a meticulous historian, Luke, who traced information from other eyewitnesses, (3) proof that these eyewitness accounts were written during the lifetimes of other eyewitnesses, who could have disputed the story if it weren't true.

C- Corroborated - the Bible is supported by archeology and non-Christian ancient writings, including anti-Christian authors.

T- Thousands - we have thousands of early manuscripts of the Bible. No other document from antiquity can compare. With these documents, textual scholars can confirm with 99.5% accuracy what the original New Testament documents said, and it's been confirmed that the 0.5% impacts no doctrine of the Christian faith.

The Bible is CORRECT. Thus, it is helpful to point out that men can't predict the future, but the author of the Bible can. We've discussed various prophecies that were recorded centuries before Jesus was born, yet He fulfilled them. How can this be if the author of the Bible was simply a man? With all of our advanced technology today, we have a 50/50 chance of predicting a 10-day weather forecast correctly. So we know that man cannot predict the future, and we know that the author of the Bible is not a man.

Brothers and Sisters in Christ, I urge you not to let concerns about attacks on the Bible deter you from sharing the Gospel. Jesus has commanded *all* of His followers to share the good news, not only those who have gone to Bible College. Plus, the Bible doesn't need to be defended by you, anyway! The Word of God is active and alive, sharper than any double-edged sword.[116] As Charles Spurgeon put it, "The Word of God is like a lion. You don't have to defend a lion. All you have to do is let the lion loose, and the lion will defend itself."

Chapter 17

WHY DOES GOD ALLOW SO MUCH EVIL AND SUFFERING?

B rothers and Sisters in Christ, your ability to address this challenging question is a powerful tool on your Gospel-sharing tool belt. I regularly receive comments on social media like these:

> *"If he exists why does he allow so much hate n murder n crime in his so-called loved children?"*

> *"What kind of God allows kids to get cancer and murders to occur? A sick god."*

Now, this "problem of evil" is a worthy question to tackle for both Christians and agnostics. It is important, however, to understand that the existence of evil is a truly absurd reason for an atheist to use as justification for rejecting the God of the Bible.

According to atheists, God does not exist. They believe we are cosmic accidents with no ultimate purpose in the universe. So, what exactly is the problem with a purposeless accident of nature being hungry or killed? Why should anyone care? In an atheistic worldview, there is no good or evil. Dr. Richard Dawkins, the poster child for modern atheists, puts it this way, "The universe that we observe has precisely the properties we should expect if there is, at bottom, no design, no purpose, no evil, no good, nothing but pitiless indifference." That is atheism in a nutshell. The Holocaust, slavery, and even terrorism, in their worldview, aren't evil. They believe that things just happen, you die, and then you're gone.

So, when an atheist says something like, "*Tell that to all the starving children in the developing world that God seems to have forgotten about*" – their conscience is revealing the hypocrisy of their purported beliefs. Their moral indignation is a direct contradiction to their stated worldview. Why are they upset if they believe these starving children are meaningless overgrown germs? It is, in fact, evidence that they are suppressing the truth of God as stated in Romans 1:18. *The wrath of God is being revealed from heaven against all the godlessness and wickedness of people, who suppress the truth by their wickedness, since what may be known about God is plain to them, because God has made it plain to them.*

This argument is summarized exquisitely by former atheist CS Lewis. "My argument against God was that the universe seemed so cruel and unjust. But just how had I got this idea of just and unjust? A man does not call a line crooked unless he has some idea of a straight line. What was I comparing this universe to when I called it unjust? If the whole show was so bad and senseless, so to speak, why did I, who was supposed to be a part of the show, find myself in such a violent reaction against it?"

There is another book in this series: You Don't Need a Ph.D. to Find G-O-D. It goes deeper into the evidence for why we believe God exists.

But for our purposes here, we're just pointing out that the problem of evil presupposes that God exists. So now, let's tackle it!

The "problem of evil" is an issue that everyone can relate to because our world is overwhelmed with pervasive evil and suffering everywhere. This includes:

- *Natural evil-* everything from disease and natural disasters to the aging process. It reflects that we are living in a fallen world.

- *Moral evil-* this is the wickedness and sin that dominates humanity. We know that sin is inevitable for every one of us. This implies that every human interaction is a collision of multiple evil sinners. Is it any wonder, then, that relationships malfunction?

- *Supernatural evil-* this includes demonic evil and false religious systems. Ephesians 6 touches on this, "For our struggle is not against flesh and blood, but against the rulers, against the authorities, against the powers of this dark world and against the spiritual forces of evil in the heavenly realms."[1]

All of this begs the question: if God is all-powerful, all-knowing, and good like the Bible says He is, then why does He allow this stuff to happen?

Some well-intentioned Christians are tempted to try to get God off the hook for all of this evil. So, you'll hear rationale like, "God isn't responsible for it; Adam and Eve are." Or perhaps, "God isn't responsible for it, the devil is." These aren't great answers because Adam, Eve, and even Satan were all created by our one true living God. So, it comes back to Him. Others attempt to rationalize evil by limiting God in some way. For example, they may limit His knowledge of the evil that is going to occur or limit His power to be able to stop the evil in the world. This limitation is sometimes presented as God not wanting to interfere with our free will. But, again, while usually well-intentioned, these aren't great answers because they're simply not what the Bible teaches.

My friend, I have good news for you. You can take "getting God off the hook for the evil in the world" off your to-do list because he's not looking to be let off the hook. **In fact, the authoritative Word of God makes it crystal clear that God is unhesitatingly sovereign over everything that exists, including evil.** [118] Does this sound like a God who is distancing Himself from being in charge?

> *I am the Lord and there is no other; I form the light and create darkness, I make peace and create calamity; I, the Lord, do these things.*[119]

> *The Lord kills and makes alive; He brings down to the grave and brings up, the Lord makes poor and makes rich; He brings low and lifts up; He raises the poor from the dust And lifts the beggar from the ash heap, to set them among princes And make them inherit the throne of glory. For the pillars of the Earth are the Lord's, And He has set the world upon them.*[120]

> *If there is calamity in a city, will not the Lord have done it?*[121]

> *All the inhabitants of the earth as reputed as nothing; He does according to His will in the army of heaven And among the*

inhabitants of the Earth. No one can restrain His hand Or say to Him, "What have you done?" [122]

Now see that I, even I, am He, And there is no God besides Me; I kill and I make alive; I wound and I heal; Nor is there any who can deliver from My hand. [123]

So the Lord said to him, "Who has made man's mouth? Or who makes the mute, the deaf, the seeing, or the blind? Have not I, the Lord?[124]

Yours, O Lord, is the greatness, The power and the glory, The victory and the majesty; For all that is in heaven and in earth is Yours; Yours is the kingdom, O Lord, and You are exalted as head over all. [125]

Scripture clearly shows God has the comprehensive power to do everything and anything He wants to do. God is holy, good, all-powerful, all-knowing, all-loving, and completely sovereign. Yet, the world He created, the world we inhabit, is full of evil. How do we reconcile this?

Here is the answer:

God allows evil agents to work and then overrules evil according to His own wise and Holy plan.[126] Ultimately, He is able to make all things- including all the evil

of all time- work together for (1) the greater good of His people and (2) His glory.

There is a lot there, so let's draw out some key points:

Evil proceeds only from the creature – never from the Creator. *All* evil is committed in rebellion against our Holy God and his Holy law. God is neither the author of nor the approver of evil. On the contrary, He is "Holy, holy, Holy" – separate from everything that is sinful and evil. *God is light and in Him there is no darkness at all.*[127]

Evil is not a disruption to God's eternal plan. He isn't scrambling around trying to figure out a "Plan B."

God has a good and morally sufficient reason for all evil He allows.[128] Evil is allowed for the greater good of His people and His own glory.

Follow me as we apply this answer to the single most vile, rebellious, and evil event in history: the crucifixion of Jesus Christ.

Our Holy, sinless Lord was put to death in an act of rebellion against God. However, this evil was no disruption to God's eternal plan of salvation. As discussed in Chapter 15, God had been forecasting the crucifixion since the dawn of humanity (Garden of Eden). We can read prophecies about the crucifixion that were recorded centuries before the birth of Jesus. This evil was allowed for the greater good of His people and for His glory. The greater good is the Gospel; the salvation of all who believe in Jesus Christ. The glory of God is a demonstration of His perfect attributes. As John MacArthur summed it up: "We wouldn't know God is as righteous as He is if it hadn't been for unrighteousness, we wouldn't know God is as loving as He is if it hadn't been for sin, we wouldn't know God is as holy as He is if it weren't for judgment."

There it is, friend. The most heinous act in history is no disruption to God's eternal plan, and neither is any other evil.[129] In the moment, the crucifixion was an unspeakable tragedy. But God knew the end from the beginning. Today, we light up at the sight of a cross; we decorate our homes with them, wear them on chains around our necks, get them tattooed on our bodies, and thank God for the cross. He took what the enemy meant for evil and turned it for our good.

There is immense peace that comes from understanding this truth. That doesn't mean that evil isn't going to hurt in this life. It definitely will. But we'll conclude this topic with one more reminder: we have a Savior who can sympathize with us. Jesus Christ willingly became a man and experienced all kinds of evil. He was tempted by the devil, He had friends who betrayed Him, He was assaulted, He was scorned, He was reviled, He was abandoned, He suffered, and He wept for our sake. But why would He do this willingly?

Because we are His children, and He loves us. We can bring all our pain to Jesus. He invites us to:

> *Come to me, all you who are weary and burdened, and I will give you rest. Take my yoke upon you and learn from me, for I am gentle and humble in heart, and you will find rest for your souls. For my yoke is easy and my burden is light.*[130]

Chapter 18

A GOOD ATHEIST GOES TO HELL JUST BECAUSE THEY DON'T BELIEVE IN JESUS?

So, an atheist can be a good guy and still go to hell just because they don't believe in Jesus? Sounds unfair, doesn't it? Well – we know that God is never unfair. He is holy, righteous, good, and has no flaws. Therefore, it's clear that the flaw lies in the question.

Here is the glaring problem with the question as presented: it assumes there are "good" atheists when there are none. As we've discussed, by God's holy standard, there are no "good" people at all.

As it is written, "There is no one righteous, not one."[131]

The question makes it sound as though Jesus willingly became a man, was crucified, suffered, bore our sins, and died a substitutionary death... for people who were innocent all along. Does that make sense? Of course not. Innocent people don't need to be saved. As Jesus said, "*It is not the healthy who need a doctor, but the sick. I have not come to call the righteous, but sinners to repentance.*"[132]

Jesus didn't come into a world full of innocent people. He came into a world that was already under the condemnation of God. He didn't come into a world of people who *deserve* to spend eternity with God in heaven. He came into a world of sinners who deserve to spend eternity in hell. The Bible says the wages of sin is death[133] and that sin has been inevitable for *all* of us since The Fall.

> *This is the verdict: Light has come into the world, but people loved darkness instead of light because their deeds were evil.*[134]

Jesus came to save and not condemn anyone who doesn't believe in Him. We were already condemned because we're sinners.

> *For God did not send His Son into the world to condemn the world, but to save the world through Him.*[135]

I find the following illustration helpful in explaining this concept. When we sin, it's the equivalent of jumping out of a plane with no parachute. We're headed for certain demise, but because God is Holy and loving, He offers us a parachute (Christ) to put on. We have absolutely no capacity to save ourselves. Now - consider whether this complaint makes sense- "I'm going to die just because I won't put the parachute on?" No – you're going to die because you chose to jump out of the plane (sin). But you can be saved if you accept the free gift of the parachute (Christ).

Clearly, those who reject Jesus (their parachute) receive what they deserve: spending eternity in hell. We know that there are people who have never even heard the name of Jesus. So, essentially the question is, "Will God condemn a person for not responding to evidence that they never had?"[136] Of course not. That would make God immoral, which we know He's not. He is Holy, righteous, and good. We see in the Bible that God judges people based on the evidence that they have. And every one of us has evidence:

> *The wrath of God is being revealed from heaven against all the godlessness and wickedness of people, who suppress the truth by their wickedness, since what may be known about God is plain to them, because God has made it plain to them. For since the creation of the world God's invisibly qualities- his eternal power and divine nature- have been clearly seen, being understood from what has been made, so that people are without excuse. For although they knew God, they neither glorified Him as God nor gave thanks to Him, but their thinking became futile and their foolish hearts were darkened. Although they claimed to be wise, they became fools and exchanged the glory of the immortal God for images made to look like a mortal human being and birds and animals and reptiles.*[137]

The existence of God is made plain to us through His creation and by virtue of our having a conscience. So, when we choose to sin anyway, we are *without excuse.* No one is condemned because they didn't respond to evidence that they never had. They are condemned because they are sinners, and God is holy. They're condemned, but they're not hopeless!

For God so loved the world that He gave His one and only son, that whoever believes in Him shall not perish but have eternal life.[138]

One final scenario that comes up often on this topic is whether aborted babies are saved. Obviously, they have no capacity to believe. Yet, God, in His grace, saves the little ones that die (infants and aborted babies). In Mark 10, Jesus says, "permit the little children to come to me and forbid them not, for of such is the kingdom of heaven." And then He blesses the little ones, which is only done for people who are a part of the kingdom of God.[139]

Brothers and Sisters in Christ – are there interesting scenarios for us to consider surrounding the dissemination of the Gospel? Certainly. But we must not bury the lede.

The fact remains that there is no salvation apart from Jesus:

Jesus answered, "I am the way and the truth and the life. No one comes to the Father except through me."[140]

Salvation is found in no one else, for there is no other name under heaven given to mankind by which we must be saved.[141]

Let's look at our final instructions as followers of Christ...

Chapter 19

THE GREAT COMMISSION

Salvatore & Son's is a barber shop founded and run for decades by a charming first-generation immigrant from Italy. Today, Sal is enjoying retirement, and his two sons run the shop. It remains staffed almost exclusively with extended family.

Sal's is, in many ways, a blast from the past. A true old-school barber shop. It's a place where cash still changes hands – none of that Apple Pay or Venmo stuff. It's a place where people are greeted by name and welcomed enthusiastically with a smile. And it's a place that simply can't be replicated because it's a community that's been built over the course of 40+ years.

It's a vibrant community. The shop is basically always busy, and that's with upwards of 8 barbers cutting at any one time. I've been there early in the morning, I've been there at closing time, and I've been there at all sorts of times in between. The shop is *constantly* bustling with activity, conversation, and laughter.

That's why what happened there last week was so amazing.

I got in the chair, and, as usual, I began chatting with my barber. Mark and I have had a great relationship for years. The man is an expert technician at his craft, an extremely hard worker, and also just a warm and friendly guy. I still remember my first visit to the shop when he asked me how I usually get my hair cut. As I began to explain the type of haircut I usually got, he cut me off and told me – "I know what you need, James." And the rest is history.

That was years ago. I've had countless conversations in Mark's chair since then. But this one was different. He asked what I was up to, and I began talking about a project I was working on. That project is the book you hold in your hands right now.

As I began discussing what the book was about, the atmosphere in the shop started to shift...

Our conversation got interrupted by another barber who walked over with a question. Mark quickly answered and turned back to me - "Keep talking to me about this, James."

I continued walking through the elements of the Gospel that we've gone through together in this book. We discussed that the world being imperfect is perhaps the most obvious thing in history. And that this reality begs the question, "How did we get from 'God created the heaven and the earth, and it was very good' to... this?"

Next, I explained that instead of guessing, we could read. So, I shared what the Bible says about Original Sin and the Fall of Humanity. Instead of getting hung up on the metaphorical vs. literal interpretations of the account (i.e., was there really a talking snake?), we discussed how this doctrine says that sin is inevitable for all of us. Finally, I asked if he (1) knew anyone who was perfect and (2) how he'd react to the idea of streaming every thought he'd ever had on a movie screen to his friends, family, and loved ones. With this, we were on the same page about every one of us being imperfect sinners.

At about this point, Mark excitedly encouraged me to keep going. I hadn't noticed because I was holding my head still and looking in the mirror for my haircut, but the entire shop had stopped their conversations and began listening to ours. Mark couldn't believe it. "My whole shop is listening to this, James!"

That only fired me up more. So, I continued through the Gospel. I revealed to them the most terrifying truth in Scripture: that God is holy. I explained that God's holiness means that He is separate from everything sinful and evil and pointed out that we had just agreed that everyone is sinful and evil.

So, I went to the law to drive the point home. We talked about how most people you talk to believe they are going to heaven because they are a "good people." But what does that really mean? "Good" compared to who? Hitler? I explained that, according to God's holy law, you can't be good enough to "earn" heaven.

I explained that while most people are familiar with the Ten Commandments, fewer are familiar with what the Bible actually says about them. For example, they're not familiar with the fact that it says if you break a single commandment once in your life, you're guilty of all. Or that Jesus taught that it's not only the outward doing of the sin, but if you even think about sinning, you're already guilty in your heart. In other words, we have absolutely no chance of meeting God's holy standard. We'd have to be as righteous as Jesus Christ Himself. I noticed in Mark's eyes that something had changed. The realization that we can't be good enough had moved him.

Now – another one of the barbers (a nephew) commented that he was just thankful that God was so forgiving. And that's absolutely right. He is forgiving. But I explained that a good judge cannot just pardon guilty sinners. That would make Him corrupt. We also talked about how Jesus, the Prince of Peace, preached more about hell than the rest of the Bible authors combined. He constantly warned sinners to escape hell.

So, it began to fall into place – Jesus had to take the punishment for us because He is the only one qualified to do so. He is the only one who lived a perfect, sinless life - something we could never do. So, Jesus died as our sin-bearing substitute and said, "It is finished" when He accomplished the will of His Father.

By this point, my haircut was finished, and I was standing, preaching to the rest of the shop. To explain how to get the benefits of Jesus' sacrifice in our own lives, I went back to the story of Paul and Silas in prison. Their reaction to being wrongfully imprisoned for their belief in Jesus was to praise God anyway, and that night, as they praised God, the walls shook, the prison doors flew open, and their chains fell loose to the ground. The jailer was stunned and realized that killing himself would be better than what would happen to him when his Roman bosses discovered that his captives had escaped. But Paul called out to him, "Don't harm yourself. We're here." So the jailer came in, trembling, and begged. Sirs, what must I do to be saved? And Paul taught him that you simply must believe in the Lord Jesus Christ.

All men in that room, whether young or old were moved. They began to say how the message was inspiring and understandable. I told them I was grateful to hear that they were inspired, but I wanted them to understand that this is a life and death issue – a heaven and hell issue. I told them about how Greg Koukl says that we don't need to get people to the foot of the cross in every single conversation we have with people about the Gospel but that we want to be a "rock in their shoe."

And, God willing, I believe these men now have a rock in their shoes.

So – why do I share this with you, my dear Brothers and Sisters in Christ? It's to encourage you in your Great Commission. Jesus' final instruction to

His followers is to preach the Gospel! It's to make disciples of all nations, baptizing them in the name of the Father, and of the Son, and of the Holy Spirit. This is what He commanded before ascending back up into heaven to sit at the right hand of the Father in glory.

And as my Pastor likes to remind us – it's not called the "Great Recommendation." It's not something optional for followers of Christ. Commission is defined as "an instruction, command, or duty given to a person or a group of people." We are that group of people. Every one of us shares the responsibility to proclaim this message. And we get the joy of being obedient to the will of God when we do.

It is my prayer that God would use this book to equip you to preach the Gospel more effectively. Mark had spent *decades* of his life in that shop, and he was stunned when the entire place came to a halt to listen to the message. There's nothing particularly special about me. I've been in that chair countless times and had countless conversations on countless topics. Yet, not once has the entire shop stopped to listen. It's not about me - it's the power of God! The Gospel is the single greatest offer in history. It is the most powerful message to ever be announced on planet Earth. And that's the truth.

I leave you with this:

> *If you declare with your mouth, "Jesus is Lord," and believe in your heart that God raised Him from the dead, you will be saved. For it is with your heart that you believe and are justified, and it is with your mouth that you press your faith and are saved. As Scripture says, "Anyone who believes in Him will never be put to shame." For there is no difference between Jew and Gentile- the same Lord is Lord of all and richly blesses all who call on Him, for "Everyone who calls on the same of the*

Lord will be saved." How, then, can they call on the one they have not believed in? And how can they believe in the one of whom they have not heard? And how can they hear without someone preaching to them? And how can anyone preach unless they are sent? As it is written, "How beautiful are the feet of those who bring good news!"[142]

Go get 'em.

Download free printable shareable Gospel Tracts

TURN THE PAGE FOR MORE!

REVIEW REQUEST

If you enjoyed **What Exactly is the Gospel?**, I'd sincerely appreciate it if you'd leave a review. Positive reviews, even if just a sentence or two, are a huge help to search results and credibility so other people can find this book. Thank you!

Review Amazon US.
Review Amazon Canada.
Review Amazon UK.
Review Amazon Australia

God Bless!

JAMES FINKE READERS' CLUB

My free monthly email newsletter is packed with useful info to help you share the Good News of Jesus Christ with others. It contains deals and giveaways that aren't offered anywhere else, and you'll be the first to hear when new books in the series are released! Subscribers receive a welcome package that includes:

1. A free book of mine that is ONLY available to my readers' club.

2. A free audio download of the "You Don't Need a Ph.D. to Find G-O-D" message I delivered at my home church.

SUBSCRIBE

MORE BOOKS BY JAMES FINKE

H AVE YOU READ THE ENTIRE ***CHRISTIANITY UNCOM-PLICATED*** SERIES?

This book distills and deciphers the evidence that the God of the Bible exists. Are you ready? Let's talk God.

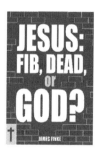

This book answers the most important question in history, asked by the most important person in history. Are you ready? Let's talk Jesus.

This book gives the business case for why we believe the Bible is the Word of God. Are you ready? Let's talk Bible.

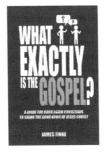

This book shares the most powerful message ever delivered on planet Earth. Let's talk Gospel.

BONUS MATERIAL

PLEASE ENJOY THIS SNEAK PEAK AT ANOTHER BOOK IN THE SERIES...

YOU DON'T NEED A PH.D. TO FIND G-O-D

God Explained in Plain Language

JAMES FINKE

INTRODUCTION

You Don't Need a Ph.D. to Find G-O-D

My wife is a social worker by trade. I'm in the insurance business, so when she and her social worker friends talk shop, it can actually sound like a foreign language to me. "*I checked on the QRC, but his DZM was ABC.*" You probably know the feeling. It could be mechanics talking cars, doctors discussing a procedure, whatever. If it's not your trade, they might as well be speaking Greek. You end up smiling and nodding, ready to move on to the next subject.

Does talking about God make you feel like an outsider listening to others "talk shop"? I'm convinced it is the case for many, whether or not they believe that God actually exists.

This is for you.

I'm not a pastor. I didn't go to seminary. Nor am I a professional scientist. Indeed, I've studied their work, but I couldn't write with their perspective even if I wanted to. It's kind of like, having a friend who's really into basketball. He may know his stuff, but he still isn't going to be slam-dunking if he's 5'2. I'm just a "regular guy" with the same fundamental question as you: **How do I find God?** The answer to that one question impacts and unlocks everything else in this life:

Is there a purpose for my life? Is there an afterlife? Will I someday see my friends and relatives again that have passed away? What religion is "right"? Is there a right and wrong way to live? Should I be going to church?

Now, most people accept that it takes faith to believe in God. But do you realize that it also requires faith to believe that there is no God? Faith is "the evidence of things we cannot see."[143]Right in the definition, we see that faith isn't meant to be blind. Just as our muscles can grow stronger through exercise, our faith to believe or not believe, can grow stronger through the study of the evidence.

This book is the result of my own study of the evidence. I've read, and I've listened to everything I could get my hands on from the top experts in the field. Experts in science, philosophy, history, religion, communication, and even crime investigation.

I've boiled it down and will share my takeaways as only a "regular guy" can. For example, I'll reference expert scientific research, but we won't get bogged down in hyper-technical scientific discussion. I'll also avoid using religious terms that would likely be foreign to those outside of the church.

I'm giving you the bottom line here and will share sources you can use to dive deeper into any of the topics we hit. If you want to know the intricacies of the second law of thermodynamics or to explore deep anagogical hermeneutics, there are plenty of places you can get that; it just won't be in this book.

Are you ready? Let's talk God.

ABOUT THE AUTHOR

James Finke has spent the past 15+ years in Corporate America managing $50-million-dollar insurance portfolios. He is an expert in assessing risk and hedging bets. Therefore, it sometimes catches people off-guard when they discover he has gone all-in and wagered *everything* that the Bible is true.

His writing ministry began as a "quarantine project" for his church back in 2020. It has developed into a book series with thousands of copies in 13 countries and counting. The ultimate goal of the ministry is to glorify God and share the Gospel. Therefore, 100% of book proceeds are poured right back into advertising the *Christianity Uncomplicated* series around the world.

James lives with his wife and three young kids in Connecticut. He hosts a vibrant community of thousands of Christ-followers on his author page on TikTok. You can follow him at https://www.tiktok.com/@authorjamesfi

nke. You can also join the thousands of Christians who connect with James on email by signing up for his author newsletter at authorjamesfinke.com

1. Matthew 9: 35-38 NKJV

2. Fox News 03/22/2022

3. Businessinsider.com

4. Genesis 3 NKJV

5. Romans 5:12, 18, 19 NKJV

6. Genesis 6:5 NKJV

7. Pastor Paul Washer

8. Romans 3:10 NIV

9. Romans 7:15, 18-20 NIV

10. Paul Washer

11. Galatians 1: 8-9 NKJV

12. Luke 11:1-4 ESV

13. Habbakuk 1:13 NASB

14. Deuteronomy 32:4 NKJV

15. Psalm 97:2 AMP

16. 1 John 1:5

17. Isaiah 59:2 NIV

18. Ecclesiastes 3:11 NIV

19. Psalm 5:4 NKJV

20. Pew Research Center

21. Gospel Coalition

22. Matthew 25:41-46 NKJV

23. Matthew 5: 27-30 AMP

24. Matthew 8:12 NKJV

25. Matthew 10:28 NKJV

26. Matthew 5:22 NKJV

27. 2 Corinthians 10:12 NKJV

28. Psalm 50:21 NKJV

29. Luke 16:15 NKJV

30. John MacArthur

31. Exodus 20: 1-17

32. Ecclesiastes 12:13 NIV

33. James 2:10 NIV

34. Romans 4:15 NIV

35. Galatians 3:10 NIV (Paul quoting Deuteronomy 27:26)

36. Kuehen – iWorld book

37. Matthew 5: 27-28 NIV

38. Galatians 3:19

39. Matthew 5:17

40. Matthew 5:48 NIV

41. Romans 3:20 NIV

42. Romans 2:14-15

43. Romans 5:20

44. Galatians 2:16

45. Coined by Pastor Paul Washer

46. Habbakuk 1:13 NIV

47. Psalms 5:5 NASB

48. Isaiah 61:8 NIV

49. Hebrews 9:27 NIV

50. Romans 2:5 NIV

51. Caselaw.findlaw.com

52. Chicago Tribune

53. Judiciaryreport.com

54. Pastor Paul Washer

55. Romans 6:23

56. Romans 3

57. Proverbs 17:15 NIV

58. Psalm 103:12 NIV

59. 77 FAQs about God and the Bible- Josh McDowell and Sean Mc-Dowell

60. Romans 3:25-26 NIV

61. Romans 6:23

62. Isaiah 53:5

63. Romans 4:25, emphasis mine

64. Romans 5:17-20 NIV

65. Matthew 11:28-30

66. Mark 16:19

67. John 5:22

68. Isaiah 1:18 NKJV

69. Acts 16: 20-24 NKJV

70. Acts 16:25

71. Acts 16:26 NKJV

72. Acts 16:27-28 NKJV

73. Acts 16:29 NKJV

74. Acts 16:31 NKJV

75. James 2:19 NIV

76. Acts 4:12

77. John 14:6

78. Galatians 3:11 NIV

79. Ephesians 2:8 NIV
80. 1 Corinthians 1:18
81. Philippians 1:6 NKJV
82. John MacArthur- The Doctrine of Repentance
83. Ezekiel 36:24-27 NIV
84. Hebrews 12: 7-11 NIV
85. Ezekiel 36: 20-23 NIV
86. Matthew 7:16 NIV
87. John 3:1-18 NIV
88. Romans 6:23 NIV
89. 2 Corinthians 5:17 NKJV
90. Ephesians 2:10 NKJV
91. James 1:18 NKJV
92. Pastor John MacArthur
93. Matthew 7:7 NIV
94. Luke 23: 32-49 NIV
95. Romans 6: 3-7 NIV
96. Acts 16: 29-31 NIV
97. Acts 2:41 NIV
98. John 14:6 NIV
99. John 14:6 NIV
100. Acts 4:8-12 NIV
101. Galatians 6: 1-10 NKJV
102. 1 Cor 15:14 NIV
103. One Solitary Life
104. Matthew NIV Intro

105. Matthew 1:22 NIV

106. Matthew 8:16 NIV

107. Matthew 2:3-6 NIV

108. Matthew 13:34 NIV

109. John 20: 30-31 NIV

110. Luke 24: 25-27 NKJV

111. Romans 1:2 NKJV

112. See Acts 2: 14-39

113. Genesis 3: 14-15 NKJV

114. Psalm 22 NIV

115. YouTube: Wretched: Atheist Objection: The Bible is unreliable because it's written by men.

116. Hebrews 4:12 NIV

117. Ephesians 6:12 NIV

118. John MacArthur: The Problem of Evil

119. Isaiah 45:7 NIV

120. 1 Samuel 2: 6-8 NIV

121. Amos 3:6 NKJV

122. Daniel 4:35 NKJV

123. Deuteronomy 32:39 NKJV

124. Exodus 4:11 NKJV

125. 1 Chronicles: 29:11 NKJV

126. John MacArthur: The Problem of Evil

127. 1 John 1:5 NIV

128. Jeff Durbin- The Problem of Evil

129. Genesis 50:20

130. Matthew 11:28 NKJV

131. Romans 3:10 NKJV

132. Luke 5:31 NIV

133. Romans 6:23 NKJV

134. John 3:19

135. John 3: 16-17

136. John Lennox- What about those who have never heard?

137. Romans 1: 18-23 NIV

138. John 3:16 NIV

139. John MacArthur- Do aborted babies go to heaven?

140. John 14:6 NIV

141. Acts 4:12 NIV

142. Romans 10: 9-15 NIV

143. Hebrews 11:1 NKJV

Made in the USA
Middletown, DE
03 December 2023

44290102R00075